CW01083591

British Railways
The First 25 Years

Volume 9
London

The London Midland Region
including the London, Tilbury & Southend Line

The second of the two LM&SR-designed main line diesel-electrics, No. 10001, parked between a brake tender and Sulzer Type '2' No. D5080 at Willesden, probably in 1963. After delivery of the English Electric Type '4's from 1958 onwards, No. 10001 was used on local freight work and other secondary duties from around late 1959 until its withdrawal in March 1966. It still has its original raised cast aluminium alloy numbers and waist stripe and received yellow warning panels in October 1962. No. D5080 entered service in March 1960 and was allocated to Willesden, then D01 London Division until December 1966 when it was transferred to the Stoke Division. Until the London Midland electrification was completed at the end of 1965, the Willesden Type '2's worked on suburban and parcels services and Euston Empty Coaching Stock duties, and also on freight work.

BRITISH RAILWAYS

The First 25 Years

Volume 9 – London

The London Midland Region including the London, Tilbury & Southend Line

J. Allan and A. Murray

Lightmoor Press

Above: The suburban service between Euston and Watford was electrified by the London & North Western Railway on the 630 Volt DC third- and fourth-rail system, and electric trains began operation in July 1922. Two three-car BR-built EMUs form a service to Euston near Kenton on 5th March 1966.

Cover photographs

Front upper: The BR Sulzer Type '4' and Type '2' diesel-electrics were the mainstay of the Midland Lines out of London from the 1960s until the 1980s, supplemented for a few years by the BRC&W Type '2's. No. D120 and No. D5221 were in front of St. Pancras signal box in April 1967.

Front lower: Many young admirers record the number of 'Princess Royal' 4-6-2 No. 46203 *Princess Margaret Rose* as it prepares to depart from Euston in August 1956. It was at Crewe North between May 1953 and September 1958, when it moved to Edge Hill. After withdrawal in October 1962, it was purchased by the Butlin's Holidays company and displayed at their Pwllheli holiday camp, where it remained until 1975. No. 46203 was then moved to the Midland Railway Centre at Butterley and subsequently purchased by the Princess Royal Class Locomotive Trust and restored for main line operation in 1990. *Princess Margaret Rose* was operational until 1996 and has been on static display since then.

Back upper: The London, Tilbury & Southend was predominantly a tank engine line with LM&SR 3-cylinder 2-6-4Ts taking over the bulk of the passenger duties from the LT&SR 4-4-2Ts in the mid-1930s. After the war they were joined by Fairburn and BR Standard 2-6-4Ts and together operated the commuter service out of Fenchurch Street until steam was swept away by electrification in 1962. No. 42514 departs from Laindon with a Shoeburyness train in 1961. It left the LT&S during the Second World War, firstly in 1942 moving to Leicester and then on to Kentish Town for six months in late 1944 before returning to Shoeburyness where it remained until withdrawal in April 1962.

Back centre: 'AL6' No. E3162 about to depart from Euston on 29th March 1967. It was one of 100 new electric locomotives delivered for the electrification between Crewe and Euston which was completed in November 1965.

Back lower: Half a mile north of Elstree station, '8F' 2-8-0 No. 48721 heads south past Milepost 13 with a typical load of coal from the East Midlands coalfields. No. 48721 was built at Brighton Works for the L&NER in 1946 and had three different numbers before it was taken into LM&SR stock as No. 8721 in late 1947. This picture was taken while it was allocated to Wellingborough, between November 1950 and May 1953 when it moved to Stourton. There are just five steel-bodied wagons in the train (plus one van!); the remainder of the fifty-odd wagons are all ex-Private Owner minerals in various states of disrepair – clearly a new build programme was needed.

Designed by Stephen Phillips.

British Library Cataloguing-in-Publication Data.
A catalogue record for this book is available from the British Library.
ISBN 978-1-911038-72-6

LIGHTMOOR PRESS
Unit 144B, Lydney Trading Estate, Harbour Road,
Lydney, Gloucestershire GL15 4EJ
www.lightmoor.co.uk

Lightmoor Press is an imprint of
Black Dwarf Lightmoor Publications Ltd.

Printed in Poland
www.lfbookservices.co.uk

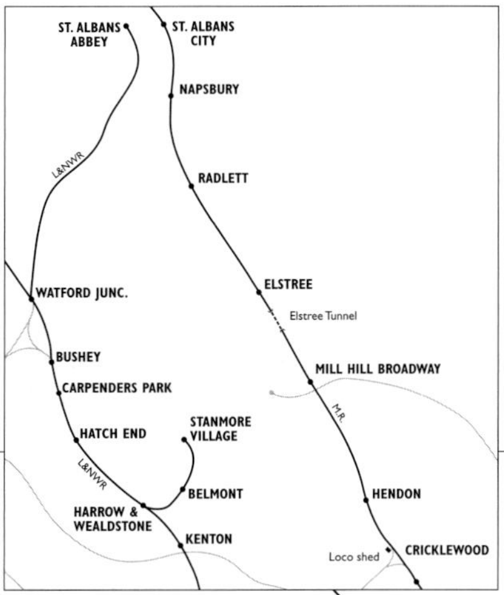

The pictures in this book illustrate the London Midland Region lines from London including St. Pancras and Euston and outlying stations out to Watford and St. Albans. Also covered is the North London Line and the London, Tilbury & Southend Line from Fenchurch Street to Shoeburyness.

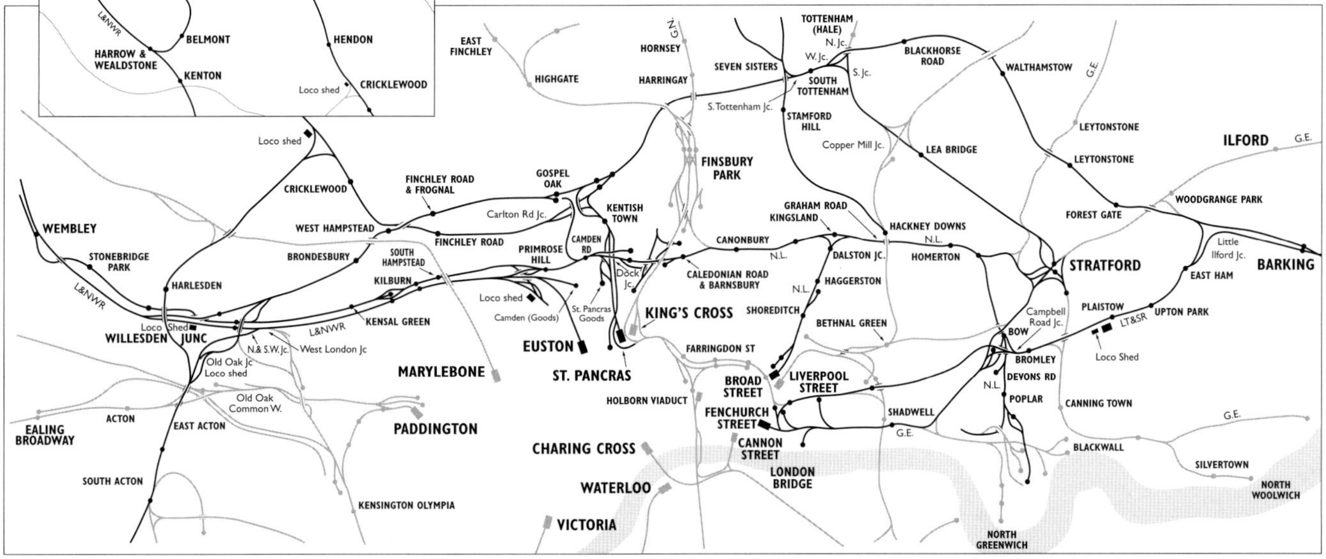

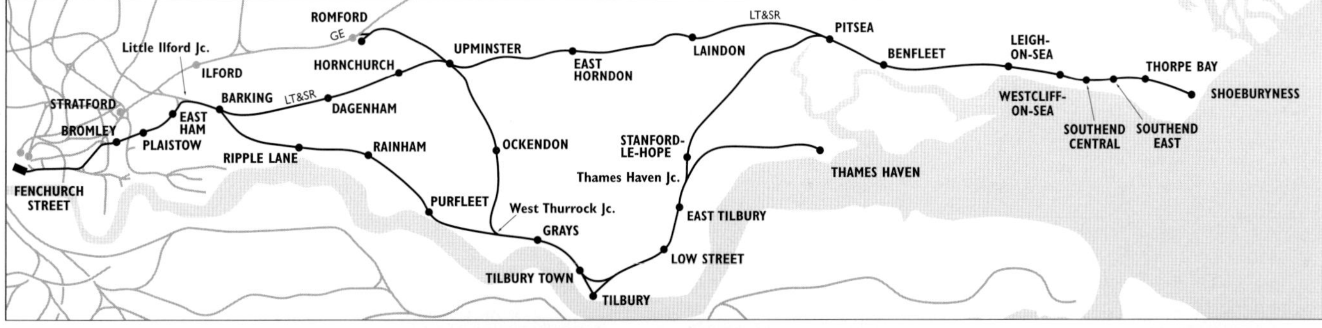

One of the BR Sulzer 'Peak' Type '4's to carry on the tradition of regimental names from the 'Royal Scot' class, No. D163 *Leicestershire and Derbyshire Yeomanry* waits for departure time at St. Pancras with the 11.20 to Leicester on Christmas Eve 1966. It was named at Derby Midland station on 14th April 1962 four days before it officially entered service. No. D163 was one of a number of the class refurbished at the Brush Traction works in Loughborough during 1966 and repainted in plain green without the grey body stripe and grills. It was destined to be the last 'Peak' to retain green livery and became No. 46026 under TOPS in 1974; it was withdrawn in November 1984.

Contents

The last Stanier 'Jubilee' 4-6-0 to be built, No. 45742 *Connaught*, rushes through Harrow & Wealdstone with a northbound express on 22nd August 1959. It had been allocated to Bushbury since July 1951 but would move to Carlisle Upperby in November 1959. Note the spotters on the bridge and the sloping embankment on the right, behind the 'Gentlemen' sign.

Introduction and Acknowledgements

This is the ninth in a series of books, depicting the first 25 years of British Railways, which will eventually cover the whole of the UK. We have been fortunate to have had access to hundreds of different pictures from which to choose the final selection presented here. At an early stage, we made the decision to include photographs spanning the early British Railways era through to the pre-TOPS diesels and electrics, although the emphasis is on that interesting transitional period of the late 1950s and early 1960s.

This volume covers the London Midland Region lines in the London area, from the terminus stations at Euston and St. Pancras out as far as Watford and St. Albans respectively, the North London Line from Broad Street and the former London, Tilbury & Southend Railway (LT&SR) lines out of Fenchurch Street. We devote a number of pages to the steam age Euston Station and its rebuilding for the West Coast electrification in the 1960s.

We visit the four principal motive power depots serving the Western and Midland Divisions, Camden, Willesden, Cricklewood and Kentish Town, and also Devons Road on the North London Line and Ripple Lane, Plaistow, Tilbury and Shoeburyness on the London Tilbury & Southend.

On the Western Division expresses 'Jubilees', 'Royal Scots' and Stanier 'Pacifics' gave way to English Electric Type '4's which followed in the footsteps of the prototype diesels that ran on the Region in the 1950s. The diesels were short-lived and were ousted by electric traction from the end of 1965. Freight was still handled by ex-L&NWR 0-8-0s alongside a relatively small number of '4F' 0-6-0s and '8F' 2-8-0s which eventually gave way to Type '1' and '2' diesels. The local trains to Watford had been electrified since 1922 and only changed when new BR-designed units were introduced in the late 1950s. The steam suburban traffic was worked by 2-6-4Ts of both Fowler and Stanier varieties, and then by Type '2' diesels before 'AM10' electric multiple units took over in 1966.

Out of St. Pancras, 'Jubilees' and 'Royal Scots' were replaced by 'Peak' diesel-electrics which, along with Sulzer and BRC&W Co. Type '2's, also took over most of the main line freight from the '8F's and 0-6-0s. The Fowler and Stanier 2-6-2Ts were ousted by Rolls-Royce-engined diesel multiple units which worked on the suburban services for a quarter century once they had overcome their initial teething problems. There was a brief period of glamour in the early 1960s with the 'Midland Pullman' service to Manchester which contrasted with the ignominy of the 'Metro-Vick' Co-Bos which were quickly banished to the north west after a very brief and unsuccessful spell on passenger and express freight work.

On the North London Line the uniformity of the EMU-worked passenger services from Broad Street to Watford and Richmond contrasted with the variety of steam classes on cross-London freights. The LT&SR was no backwater of the LM&SR but was its busiest commuter line into the Capital and there was also a healthy summer traffic of day trippers, primarily to Southend. Until its electrification in 1962 the 'Tilbury' was almost exclusively a tank engine line with the LT&SR-designed 4-4-2Ts working alongside the LM&SR 2-6-4Ts on the intensive steam-hauled passenger services from Fenchurch Street for the first few years after nationalisation.

As with the previous London volumes, we have included detailed maps with the location of the principal stations and depots showing how they fit into the Capital's streets. Platform layouts are also provided for each of the termini.

Acknowledgements

Once again, we are grateful for the expertise and enthusiasm of Steve Phillips who designed this book as well as our previous volumes in this series. Our thanks also go to Vic Smith for his help. Any errors remaining are of course entirely the responsibility of the authors.

The majority of the pictures in this volume are from the *www.Rail-Online.co.uk* collection including many from Rail Archive Stephenson. In the chapter on Euston station we have used a number of photographs from the Ben Brooksbank collection under the Creative Commons licence. We have taken the opportunity to include many whole page portraits which show the quality of some of these fifty or sixty-year old photographs.

References

We have consulted a number of books to provide details of locomotives and workings. In particular, the RCTS BR Standard and LM&SR series and *The Allocation History of BR Diesels & Electrics* have allowed us to include full details of allocations. One book has been particularly helpful, *London's Termini* by A. A. Jackson as have Peter Kay's series of books on the London, Tilbury & Southend.

J. Allan and A. Murray 2019

1 – Euston

Euston was the first main line terminus in London when it was opened by the London & Birmingham Railway in July 1837. The line was originally planned to terminate at Camden but before completion it was extended to Euston Grove, 1¼ miles nearer to London. Construction of this section involved crossing Regent's Canal and then descending steeply at between 1 in 68 and 1 in 77. The lightweight steam locomotives of the time were not up to the task of hauling trains up an incline of this magnitude and therefore trains were hauled by rope up to Camden, a practice which continued until 1844.

Euston station was enlarged and modernised several times in the century before it was completely rebuilt for the LMR electrification in the 1960s. In addition to numerous enhancements to the facilities and offices, between 1869 and 1874 two new platforms (1 and 2) were added and the original 1837 roof was raised by 6ft to improve the dispersal of smoke. Increased traffic required still more platforms and in 1892 four new departure platforms (12-15) were opened on the western side. This marked the maximum size of the old station: arrivals used Platforms 1 to 3, suburban trains 4, 5 and 7. Platform 6 was used for both arrivals and departures including the 'West Coast Postal' and royal trains, Platforms 8 to 10 mainly handled parcels traffic, Platform 11 was used for parcels, milk and fish traffic with main line departures from Platforms 12 to 15; there were also several engine sidings.

The first of several schemes for complete reconstruction was considered in 1898-9, but nothing came of this and the only significant developments were improvements to the approach lines and the construction of two new carriage sheds, one on either side of the tracks. A new double track line was built for engine movements between the terminus and Camden shed, and a tunnel built to carry an Up engine line and a Down empty carriage line from the arrival side to the carriage sidings and shed on the west side of the approach tracks. When the work was completed in 1906, four running lines became available.

The suburban service to Watford was electrified on the 630 Volt direct current (DC) third- and fourth-rail system, and electric trains began operation in July 1922, using Platforms 4, 5 and 7. Ambitious plans were drawn up by the LM&SR in the late 1930s to redevelop the station which would even have had the capacity to absorb the traffic using St. Pancras, but the outbreak of war in 1939 put paid to the scheme.

Under British Railways, the track layout was remodelled in 1952, requiring the demolition of one of the two Ampthill Square bridges and the No. 2 signal box. Thirteen diamond crossings were removed as the layout was simplified and six platforms were lengthened. A new signal box was opened in October 1952 controlling colour-light signals and electro-pneumatic points. The last changes to the old station came in 1954-5 when Platforms 12 to 15 were re-positioned and widened.

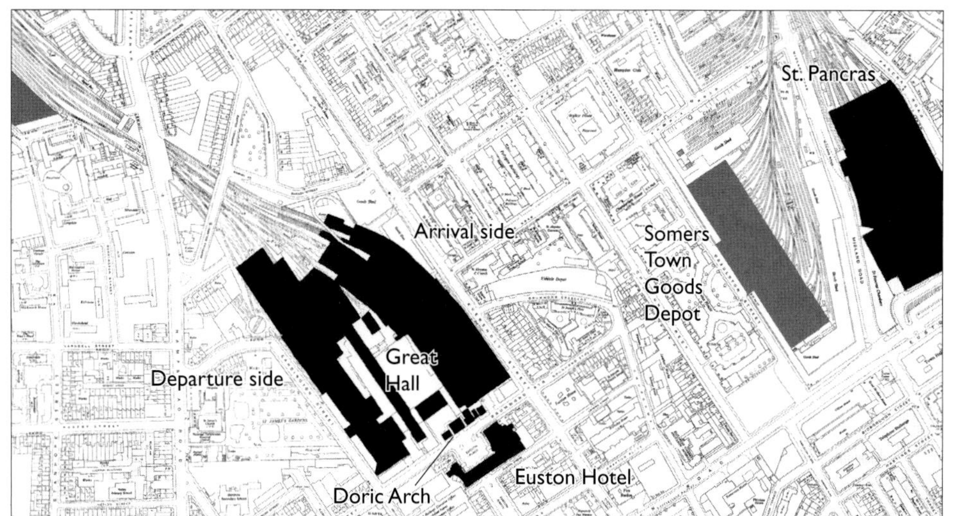

Left: Euston location map showing the station layout after Ampthill Square South Bridge had been removed but still showing the No. 2 signal box.

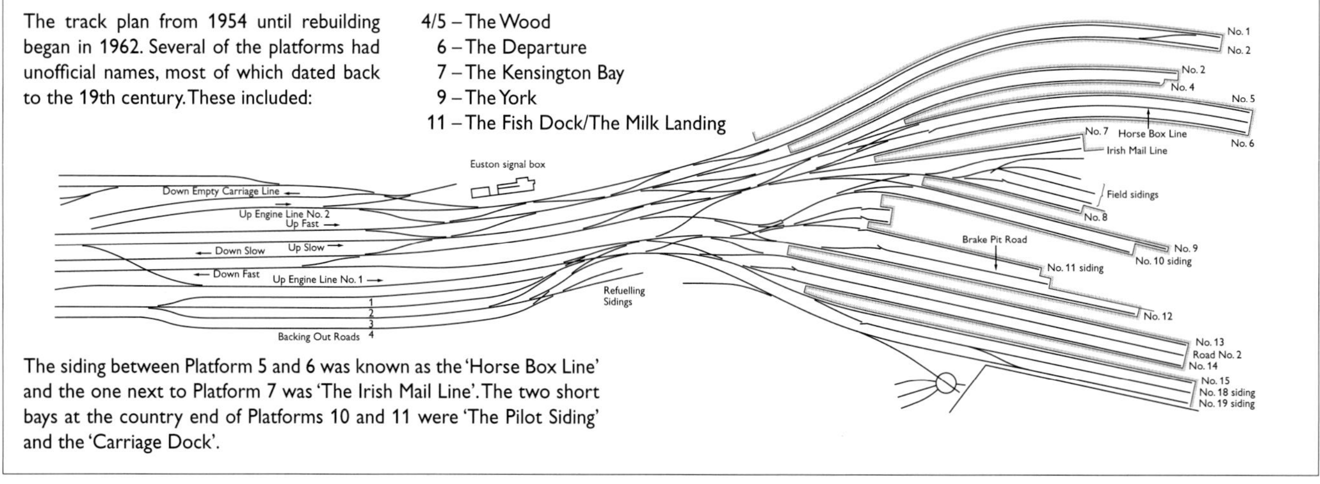

The track plan from 1954 until rebuilding began in 1962. Several of the platforms had unofficial names, most of which dated back to the 19th century. These included:

4/5 – The Wood
6 – The Departure
7 – The Kensington Bay
9 – The York
11 – The Fish Dock/The Milk Landing

The siding between Platform 5 and 6 was known as the 'Horse Box Line' and the one next to Platform 7 was 'The Irish Mail Line'. The two short bays at the country end of Platforms 10 and 11 were 'The Pilot Siding' and the 'Carriage Dock'.

The station before rebuilding

The Doric Arch and Great Hall

The ultimate symbol of the old Euston, the Doric Arch was 72ft high and was supported on four hollow columns 44ft 2in. high and 8ft 6in. in diameter.

It was a true propylaeum (defined in ancient Greek architecture as a porch or gatehouse at the entrance of a sacred enclosure) and was actually bigger than those in Athens.

The Arch was designed by the renowned architect Philip Hardwick and was completed in May 1838 by the London & Birmingham Railway at the then enormous cost of £35,000, a sum that attracted much criticism at the time. At either side of the portico were two lodges, one joined to the portico and the other separated by wrought iron gates, together forming a 300ft long screen in front of the station. The Euston name was carved into the architrave in around 1870.

Note that it forms the exit from the station, inwards traffic passing between the western lodges.

The Great Hall, a combined concourse and waiting room, was designed by Charles Hardwick, Philip's son and was completed in May 1849. It was strangely positioned in such a way that it virtually split the station into two separate parts, preventing anything other than the building of short length platforms behind it.

The Great Hall was 125ft 6in. long by 61ft 4in. wide and 62ft high. It had a curved double staircase in stone leading to a 16ft wide vestibule and a gallery round the walls. Beyond the 1852 marble statue of George Stephenson were offices, a boardroom and a shareholders' meeting room. This picture was taken on a Sunday and there were relatively few people around. *Ben Brooksbank*

It is ten-past-one in the afternoon and the Great Hall is again only sparsely populated in this view from the gallery behind the Stephenson statue. In each corner there were plaster bas-reliefs depicting the main cities and towns served by the railway. Two of these are just visible at the top of the picture, on either side of the windows.

The signs on the right are for the 'Bar' and the 'Cafeteria'; the door in the right corner led to the 'Post Office' and those in the centre to the platforms.

The Great Hall may have been loved by historians, but the facilities were wholly inadequate for the second half of the 20th century and its position prevented the construction of a modern efficient station; it simply had to go when the station was rebuilt.

The entrance

The entrance from Euston Road on 6th April 1962. Only the London & North Western Railway War Memorial and the two flanking 'classical' lodges, converted into pubs called 'The Euston Tap' and the 'East Lodge', remain today. The Doric Arch, the demolition of which had been completed in early 1962, and the station were behind the Euston Hotel, which was also a casualty of the rebuilding. There were originally two railway hotels on either side of Euston Grove which were linked in 1881 by the new hotel building in this picture, blocking off the view of the Arch which was between the hotel and the station. *Ben Brooksbank*

Two generations of the famous London 'black cab' are dropping off their fares in the courtyard off Drummond Street on 6th April 1962. In the centre is an Austin FX4 which was introduced in 1958. On either side is its predecessor the FX3 which had been built since 1948.
Ben Brooksbank

Unlike the rebuilt station, there was no segregation of pedestrians from mail/parcels road traffic.

The Arrival side

The Arrival side viewed from the road approach off Drummond Street on 6th April 1962. Platforms 1 and 2 are off to the right, Platforms 3 and 4 and the rest of the station are to the left. Note the poster advertising the 'Starlight Special' to Scotland; this ran to Edinburgh and Glasgow on Friday nights between June and September a fare of £5 return – the equivalent of around £105 today. The Second Class only service, which was designed to compete with long distance road coaches, ran between 1953 and 1962. Passengers departed overnight on Friday evening arriving on Saturday morning and returned either eight or fifteen days later on Saturday, arriving back on Sunday morning. *Ben Brooksbank*

Looking out to Drummond Street from the roadway between Platforms 1 and 2 on the left and Platforms 3 and 4 on the right. *Ben Brooksbank*

On the left, Platforms 4 and 5 with a special 'Watford Electric Line' board showing that the next train was at 10.10am from Platform 4. In the centre is arrival Platform 3, then the roadway with the taxi rank for picking up passengers and luggage, and over to the right are Platforms 2 and 1. Trolleys of mail sacks taken off an incoming train are lined up all the way down Platform 3. *Ben Brooksbank*

The Departure side

Departure Platforms 11 (left), 10, 9 and 8 (further on right) on 6th April 1962. In the centre of the picture is the 'Left Luggage Deposit' office and in the background between the signs for Platform 9 and 8 is a sign for the 'Royal Scot' bar.

Ben Brooksbank

In August 1961 the Train Departure Information shows that the train at the top departing at 3.55pm is 'The Caledonian' to Glasgow leaving from Platform 12. 'The Shamrock' will depart to Liverpool at 4.30pm from Platform 15. The list of trains is rather confusing because it contains 'Saturdays Excepted', 'Saturdays Only', etc interleaved. On the left is a fruit and confectionery kiosk run under concession by Empire Stores (Produce) Ltd.

A view towards the 'country' end of Departure Platforms 13 and 12 on 6th April 1962.

Ben Brooksbank

Rays of sunlight illuminate the view towards the barriers along Platform 12 and 13 on 6th April 1962.
Ben Brooksbank

Fowler 2-6-4T No. 42367 at Platform 14 on empty coaching stock it has brought in from Willesden on 6th April 1962. Immediately above the second coach is a bridge for road vehicles leading from Cardington Street to Platforms 11 and 10 where parcels etc. were loaded. Note the advertisements on the bridge, on the left for John Thompson Ltd of Wolverhampton who were boiler makers and engineers ('Steam for Power and Industry'), and on the right for 'Carrs – makers of fine biscuits in Carlisle for 127 years'.

Another view of No. 42367 on the same day taken from Platform 12/13 looking towards the barriers. The station is quiet at 10.35am on a Friday following the end of the morning rush-hour and the departure of the principal expresses to the north. To the left of the large clock is a poster showing one of the new LMR electric locomotives, heralding what was to come, albeit not for another four years.
Ben Brooksbank

At the end of Platform 13, Crewe North 'Coronation' 4-6-2 No. 46228 *Duchess of Rutland* is about to leave with the 10.25am to Carlisle and Windermere on 6th April 1962. With the advent of the English Electric Type '4' diesels in increasing numbers from 1959 onwards, the 'Coronations' were gradually displaced from their express duties, and by 1962 they were used mainly as stand-by express power.

Looking through Ampthill Square bridge in the mid-1950s up Camden Bank which curves away to the right. The third/fourth rail electrification of the Watford suburban lines shows up clearly. The lines were electrified at 630V DC and fed from the L&NWR-built power station at Stonebridge Park near Wembley. Current was supplied to the trains by an outer conductor rail and negative return was made by the fourth rail between the running rails. Fowler '3P' 2-6-2T No. 40068 was working on station pilot or Empty Coaching Stock duty; it was allocated to Willesden between November 1952 and withdrawal in 1959. The modern building on the left which was known as 'The Bridge' was built on the site of the old No. 2 signal box which was demolished in 1952, and housed supervisors and similar luminaries including the 'Euston Engine Arranger' who was responsible for all Motive Power activities within the station area.

1940s and early 1950s

Still with plenty of steam after its arrival at Euston, 'Coronation' Pacific No. 6233 *Duchess of Sutherland* rests alongside rebuilt 'Patriot' No. 45514 *Holyhead.* This picture was taken in mid-1948, after the 'Patriot' had been renumbered in May and before No. 6233 in September. *Duchess of Sutherland* had been fitted with smoke deflectors in August 1946 and was repainted into LM&SR 1946 lined black in October 1947. It is one of three 'Coronations' preserved and has been operating on the main line for nearly two decades. The sign immediately to the right above No. 6233 is for 'Sketchley Dry Cleaning', a business still in operation today.

The unique No. 46170 *British Legion* has lots of admirers as it gets ready to depart in 1949. It was rebuilt from the ill-fated high-pressure experimental locomotive No. 6399 *Fury* in October 1935. The latter's 'Royal Scot' type frames and motion were paired with a Stanier pattern taper boiler with Belpaire firebox to produce what became the prototype for the subsequent conversion of the whole of the 'Royal Scot' class with taper boilers from 1943 onwards. The BR number was applied in April 1948 and smoke deflectors were fitted in November 1951. Behind *British Legion* is the old Euston No. 2 signal box which was demolished in 1952 and on the left is Ampthill Square North Bridge, No. 3 in the number sequence out of Euston. Ampthill Square South No. 2 Bridge casts a shadow over the lower right of the picture.

'Coronation' No. 46240 *City of Coventry* is about to pass under Ampthill Square North Bridge as it gets underway in the early 1950s. The Pacific was de-streamlined in July 1947 and retained its sloping smokebox up to July 1953; it had BR light blue livery from January 1950 until October 1954. Note the mechanical signalling which was replaced at the end of 1952 by colour lights.

The hustle and bustle of the early 1950s Euston is noticeable as a taper boiler and a parallel boiler 'Royal Scot' rest side by side after arrival in Platforms 2 and 1 respectively. The contrast in front end appearance is very noticeable: Bushbury's No. 46110 *Grenadier Guardsman* on the right appears much more imposing than Edge Hill's No. 46135 *The East Lancashire Regiment* on the left. This picture was taken after November 1950 when No. 46135 was fitted with smoke deflectors and before July 1951 when No. 46110 was transferred away from Bushbury shed to Carlisle Upperby; *Grenadier Guardsman* was itself rebuilt with a taper boiler in January 1953. The regalia in the top left for the Festival of Britain exhibition, held between May and September 1951, confirms the date. No. 46135 had arrived first and its passengers are streaming off the train while the fireman has already changed the lamps from Express Passenger to Light Engine ready to back down to Camden shed. No. 46110 with Express Passenger headlamps has only just come to a stand and the passengers are still on the train. Note the two boards indicating the 'REFRESHMENT FACILITIES' – 'DINING ROOM', TEA ROOM', REFRESHMENT ROOM', 'REFRESHMENT BAR' and 'TEA BAR'; and, last but not least, at the foot of the sign 'TEA TROLLEYS'. The buffer stops are a special design sliding on two additional pairs of rails on either side of the running rails and designed to assist the stopping of over-zealous arriving trains. They are fitted with sockets for lamps that date back to 19th century L&NWR designs. Note also the L&NWR ground signal, painted yellow indicating permission to use the crossover from Platform 1, but not restricting an engine from following departing coaches out.

W.J.V. Anderson/Rail Archive Stephenson

One of the 1927 LM&SR-built electric units departs for Watford on 14th January 1954 while on the right a 'Jinty' shunts parcels vans. These units were introduced to cope with increased traffic in the late 1920s but, unlike the earlier L&NWR 'Oerlikon' stock which had open saloons, the passenger accommodation was in all-compartment form to speed-up station stops. Traction equipment was provided by Metropolitan Vickers, which was owned by the American GEC group, and these units became known as the 'GEC stock'.

Two schoolboy spotters are in deep conversation as they walk back from the end of the platform towards 'Princess Royal' 4-6-2 No. 46212 *Duchess of Kent*. This picture was taken after it was fitted with a domed boiler in November 1952. Ahead of the Pacific is the Ampthill Square North Bridge. Until 1952 there would also have been the Ampthill Square South Bridge which made the 'country' end of the station very restricted and claustrophobic; the North Bridge was itself removed when Euston was rebuilt in the 1960s.

'Coronation' Pacific No. 46246 *City of Manchester* basks in the Spring sunshine at Platform 1 on 11th April 1955. It was the last 'Coronation' to have a sloping top smokebox, which it kept until April 1960 even after it had received crimson lake livery in October 1958. No. 46246 had been de-streamlined in 1946 and it is surprising that the sloping smokebox lasted so long, almost two years after the previous replacement cylindrical smokebox had been fitted to No. 46243 *City of Lancaster*, which had been the last of the class to lose its streamlining, in June 1949. The signage for the 'REFRESHMENT FACILITIES' has been updated with a (less informative) British Railways enamel version since the picture on page 16. Platforms 1 and 2 were the only ones which had an engine release crossover.

Diesel prototypes

During the 1950s, Euston saw all of the prototype main line diesels, starting with the former LM&SR 'twins', Nos 10000 and 10001 and then later the three Bulleid-designed Southern Railway diesel-electrics and the English Electric *Deltic*.

The English Electric prototype 3,300bhp diesel-electric *Deltic* after arrival in Platform 2, probably in 1957. After it had been tested on the Settle & Carlisle line in late 1956, *Deltic* settled down to regular work on the London Midland Region, principally between Euston and Liverpool, which allowed English Electric engineers to travel with the locomotive on every journey. *Deltic's* day began with the 12.37am from Crewe to Euston, followed by the 7.55am from Euston to Liverpool, the 2.10pm back to London and ending with the 7.20pm to Crewe. This gave a daily mileage of 703 which the locomotive worked for six days each week.

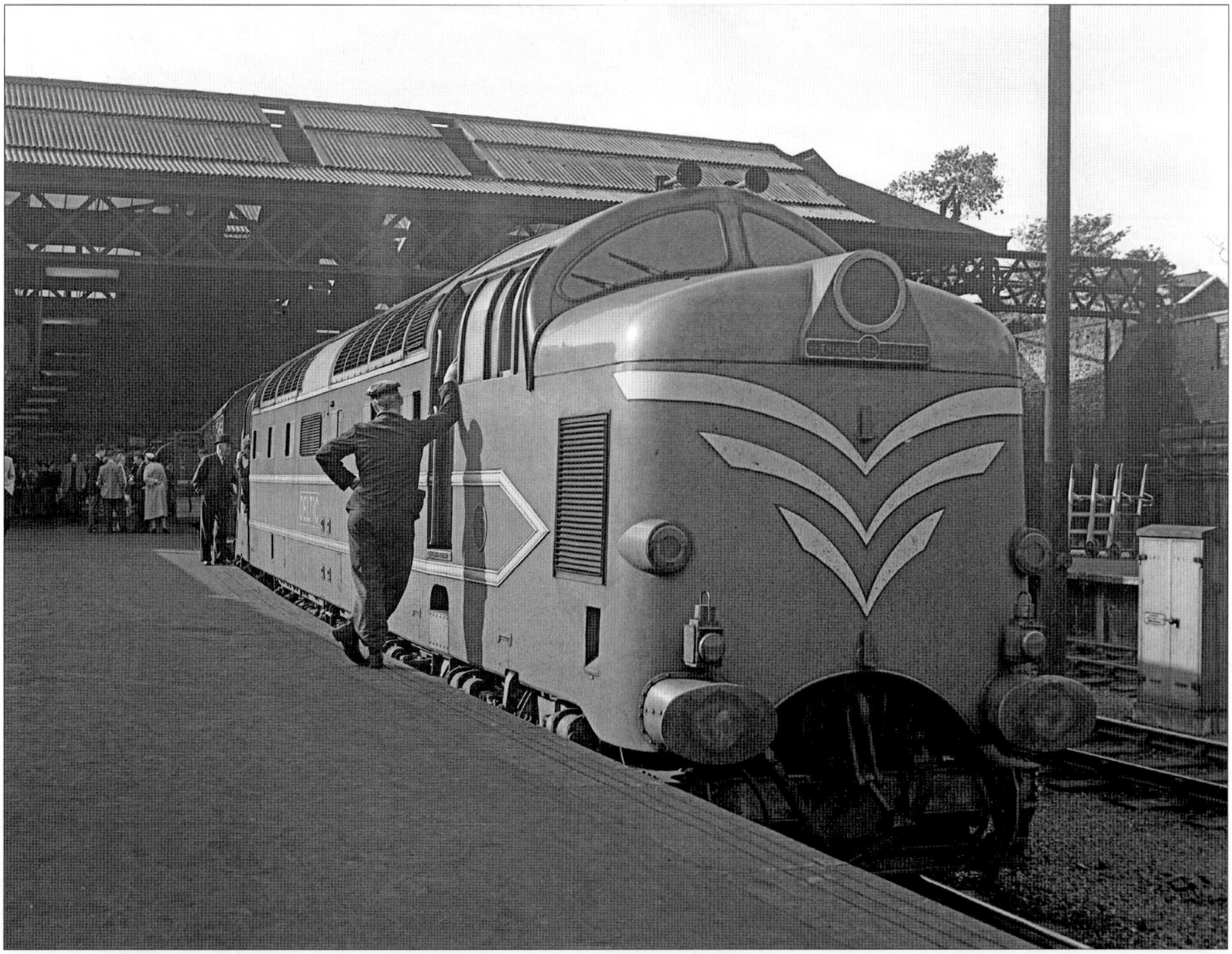

The man in the bowler hat chats with the English Electric engineer before *Deltic* departs with the 8.30am to Liverpool on 16th August 1958. In its striking pale blue livery with American style 'whiskers' and stripes, *Deltic* contrasted with the dullness prevalent in the mid-1950s. After the East Coast Regions obtained authorisation for a fleet of 'Deltics' in early 1958, the prototype was transferred there from the London Midland Region in January 1959. It worked until March 1961, overlapping by a month the first two of the production 'Deltic' series, Nos D9000 and D9001.

The Southern Railway designed a main line diesel-electric prior to nationalisation but the first one of them did not enter service until December 1950. The three locomotives, Nos 10201-3, were transferred from the Southern to the London Midland Region in 1955. No. 10203 was allocated to Camden from August 1955 until November 1959 when it moved to Willesden. It was the most powerful of the three, entering service some three years after the two earlier locomotives, and its Mark II version of the English Electric 16SVT engine was rated at 2,000bhp rather than the 1,750bhp of the Mark I. Still in its original black livery with silver lining bands and numbers, No. 10203 rests after arrival at Euston with an express from Wolverhampton on 5th May 1956. *C.R.L. Coles/Rail Archive Stephenson*

Southern Railway-designed diesel-electric No. 10203 was photographed in July 1958 at Euston when working the 'Royal Scot'. It had been repainted in British Railways green with the new style emblem after a 'Heavy General' overhaul at Derby Works which started on 23rd May 1956. No. 10203 returned to traffic on 11th January 1957, after 198 weekdays out of service. Derby had taken over the overhauls from late 1955 following its transfer to the London Midland Region from the Southern Region in April of that year. No. 10203 was the direct forerunner of the English Electric Type '4' which had the same engine and eight-wheeled bogies with one pair on each merely idle carriers of the great weight of these locomotives.

The platform-enders do not appear to be over-enthused by Britain's first main line diesel, No. 10000 which was completed only three weeks before the LM&SR was nationalised, as it runs in under Ampthill Square Bridge in 1959 or early 1960. The family resemblance of the first ten British Railways 'Peaks' to the LM&SR design is striking. This picture was taken before Overhead Warning flashes were applied during a works visit starting in August 1960. The black livery was relieved by the aluminium stock numbers which were painted cream, and the eggshell blue waist strip. No.10000 still has the '5P5F' power class which it had from August 1957 and which was changed to plain '5' in November 1960. In the late 1950s the LM&SR diesel-electric 'twins' worked singly on services from Euston to Bletchley, Birmingham/Wolverhampton and Manchester, and in multiple on the 'Royal Scot' and West Coast Main Line sleeper trains.

Note that, inevitably, the word 'Not' has been scratched out on the painted wooden 'Special Notice' board.

The last decade of steam

Arrivals

'Patriot' 4-6-0 No. 45547 and Class '5' No. 44827 arrive with an express from Blackpool on 16th May 1957. Before World War Two, the 'Patriot' 4-6-0s were used on the London-Birmingham two-hour expresses but 'Jubilee' 4-6-0s ousted them from these prestige duties in March 1939. After this, they became very much 'second division' express locomotives behind the 'Jubilees', 'Royal Scots' and Stanier Pacifics. No. 45547, which remained unnamed, was one of the final ten of the class built after William Stanier became Chief Mechanical Engineer of the LM&SR in January 1932.

T.G. Hepburn/Rail Archive Stephenson

Crewe North 'Princess Royal' 4-6-2 No. 46209 *Princess Beatrice* has steam to spare after arriving at Platform 2 in April 1960. No. 46209 was in its last full year in traffic, and along with all its classmates went into store for several months during 1961.

'Coronation' Pacific No. 46256 *Sir William A. Stanier F.R.S.* after arrival at Euston with the 'Royal Scot' from Glasgow in the summer of 1958. It was one of the last two of the class, entering service in the final month of the LM&SR before nationalisation, and incorporated a number of modifications including roller bearings on all axles, and mostly noticeably a redesigned and simpler, rear frame arrangement and cut-down cab side sheets. No. 46256 had been repainted in crimson lake livery with LM&SR style lining during a Light Intermediate works visit completed in May 1958. It was the last of the class in service, retained to work an RCTS special at the end of September 1964. In the early 1950s there was a limited return to through locomotive working between Euston and Glasgow. Scottish Region engines from Polmadie worked 'The Royal Scot' except on Sundays, Up one day and Down the next. Similarly, Camden worked the 10.8am ex-Euston and the 10.6am ex-Glasgow. Through working was unpopular with the crews who had to take over the engine for the second half of its journey when coal could become low and the ashpan full. It seems likely at this late date that No. 46256, which was a Camden engine from January 1948 until November 1959, would have taken over the train at Carlisle. Note the later tartan style train headboard with a shield depicting a Scottish (rampant) lion.

A former Western Region 'Britannia' displaced by dieselisation, No. 70029 *Shooting Star* brings in a special during 1961. The handrails on its smoke deflectors had been replaced by hand-holes on each side to improve forward visibility following an accident near Didcot with No. 70026 in November 1955. No. 70029 was transferred from Cardiff Canton to Aston in October 1961 and stayed until the end of 1964 when it went to Carlisle Kingmoor.

'Britannia' 4-6-2 No. 70042 *Lord Roberts* had moved to Willesden at the end of 1960 and was there until June 1963; the tender emblem dates from June 1961. Note the yellow-painted 'BR Timken' axlebox covers with horizontal red stripe denoting roller-bearing axleboxes.

Departures

Every year up to 1957 the British Industries Fair which promoted Britain's manufacturing industry was held at Castle Bromwich near Birmingham. With a suitably inscribed headboard, 'Jubilee' No. 45672 *Anson* heads one of the special trains put on to take visitors to the event. It was allocated to Camden from May 1949 until September 1958 apart from two short periods on loan to Bushbury in 1957.

The unique British Railways three-cylinder Caprotti Pacific No. 71000 *Duke of Gloucester* produces an impressive display of smoke and steam as it departs with 'The Mid-Day Scot' in the mid-1950s. It first worked the train between July and September 1954, resuming in May 1955 after completing trials at Swindon. No. 71000 was earmarked for preservation in the National Collection and after its early withdrawal in November 1962 was stored in Crewe Works from December 1964 until early 1967. However, it was then decided that only the Caprotti valve gear should be saved and the remainder of the engine scrapped, and so No. 71000 was sold to Woodham Brothers at Barry Docks minus its cylinders and valve gear. As is well known, that was not the end of the story and *Duke of Gloucester* was purchased for preservation in 1974 and moved to the Great Central Railway at Loughborough. During the following decade it was brought back to working order with several modifications to the engine as first built including a new ashpan and a Kylchap blast pipe. The result was a significant transformation from the engine's poor performance in BR days.

Suburban tanks

Stanier 2-6-4T No. 42478 is ready to take out the stock from a Liverpool train on 7th September 1961. It was allocated to Willesden for four years from June 1960 until June 1964. On the right of the picture is a parcels van – Platforms 8 to 11 were used for this traffic. The white enamel sign, primarily for staff not passengers, is a warning for the live rails on the adjacent lines which were used by the Watford electrics.

With rebuilding work in full swing, Fairburn 2-6-4T No. 42102 arrives at the station, probably during 1963. Originally a Southern Region engine built at Brighton, it moved to Watford in December 1959 and was there until April 1965. Note that it still has a pre-1956 BR emblem on the side tank despite the date and having received a 'Heavy General' repair in March/April 1962.

Station pilots and ECS working

Two '3F' 0-6-0Ts on station pilot duty in 1958. On the left is No. 47529 and nearest the camera is No. 47668. This was the second engine of the last batch of the class to be built, entering service as No. 16751 from Horwich Works in April 1931, and was renumbered as 7668 in 1937. Camden Shed had around fifteen of these from the 1930s onwards; these two had been there since 1931 and were among the last four to leave, both departing at the end of 1960 as Type '1' diesels took over from them.

Willesden had more than a dozen Fowler 2-6-2Ts in the mid-1950s and many of their duties were on Euston empty stock work. Auto-fitted No. 40020 was allocated there for only six months, between June 1958 and January 1959, coming from Watford where it had worked the Stanmore branch push-pull for many years.

The engine which brought in the empty stock assisted the train engine with its cold start up Camden Bank as demonstrated by BR Standard Class '2' 2-6-0 No. 78063 in August 1965. It was one of seven of the class transferred from the North West to Willesden in May 1963 in exchange for an equivalent number of the LM&SR Ivatt design, because the BR engines were fitted with AWS which was a requirement for engines working in the London area. They were used on cross-London freights and shed/yard pilot duties, and occasionally on Euston-Bletchley suburban trains and towards the end of their stay on Euston-Wembley ECS. No. 78063 was at Willesden until the depot closed in September 1965, moving to Nuneaton along with five classmates.

Ivatt Class '4' 2-6-0 No. 43018 at Euston in 1965 when, with the rebuilding of the station almost complete, the absence of watering facilities meant that ECS working had to be done by tender engines with a greater water capacity than the tank engines used previously. No. 43018 was transferred along with No. 43007 from Watford to Willesden in April 1965 and left six months later as electric services were about to begin. The class had not been seen on Euston ECS workings since September 1951 when No. 43001 was noted there shortly before it left Devons Road.

Diesels in the late 1950s/early 1960s

A BR Sulzer Type '2' waits in the 'Horse Box Line' siding between Platforms 5 and 6 in April 1961 with a Watford EMU on the left in Platform 4 and a train of BR Mark 1 Suburban coaches on the right in Platform 7. This picture was taken from Platform 3 on the Arrival side looking towards the shorter platforms 4/5 and 6/7, which were used for local trains. On the extreme left the taxi-ramp can just be seen descending between Platforms 2 and 3, having curved all the way round outside Platform 1 from Drummond Street.

BR Sulzer Type '4' No. D7 *Ingleborough* entered traffic in November 1959 and worked on the WCML until February 1962 moving to Toton when the first ten 'Peaks' were concentrated there for freight work and remained there until withdrawal. It became No. 44007 in February 1974 and was withdrawn in November 1980. The lone spotter is standing alongside the warning sign to engine spotters which had not been 'modified' at this date.

A contrast in front ends of the two Type '4' diesel-electrics introduced under the BR Modernisation Plan. On the left in Platform 2 BR Sulzer No. D7 *Ingleborough* bears a close resemblance to the LM&SR prototypes Nos 10000 and 10001 whereas the English Electric on Platform 1 which has brought in 'The Mancunian' has the less rounded nose-end which was characteristic of that company's designs. The first ten Sulzers worked alongside the English Electrics on the West Coast Main Line for around two years before they were banished to freight work in the East Midlands. They were all named after British mountains, hence the 'Peak' nickname applied by enthusiasts; Ingleborough is the second highest mountain in the Yorkshire Dales at 2,372ft high.

Large numbers of English Electric Type '4' diesel-electrics were delivered to the London Midland Region from early 1959 onwards, displacing the Stanier Pacifics from their position as the primary motive power on the West Coast Main Line. No. D219 after arrival at Euston in a photograph taken shortly after it entered service in July 1959 with a nose-end handrail and without a yellow warning panel; it was named *Caronia* in mid-1962.

The Type '1' and Type '2' diesels had a relatively short period working empty coaching stock out of Euston in the first half of the 1960s, although the Type '2's continued on parcels traffic into the late 1970s. The English Electric 1,000 bhp Bo-Bos replaced the steam station pilots at Euston and also joined the BR Sulzers on ECS and suburban work. Ex-works No. D5012 had recently been through Derby Works in mid-1963 when it gained a yellow warning panel and lost the Southern Region headcode disc brackets fitted to the cab fronts for the SR six disc headcodes. It was built in April 1959 and by the end of the month had moved to Hither Green, remaining on the Southern until May 1962 when it was transferred first to Crewe South and then Crewe North. No. D5012 arrived at Willesden in November 1963 and returned in December 1964 to Crewe North. It left the London Midland Region in 1971 for Polmadie and then Eastfield where it was withdrawn in August 1975 as No. 24012.

The overhead wires are in place but not yet live as English Electric Type '4' No. D329 departs with a Manchester express in 1965. It was delivered from Vulcan Foundry in January 1961, was renumbered as No. 40129 in 1974 and remained in service until May 1984.

Three English Electric Type '4' diesel-electrics ready to take out northbound expresses are in the background behind BR Sulzer Type '2' No. D5022 in 1965. It was one of the class allocated initially to the Eastern Region, firstly at Norwich and later to Ipswich. No. D5022 was transferred to Camden in March 1961, at first on loan and then permanently two months later; sixteen, Nos D5020-D5035, were released by the former Great Eastern depots to the LMR as new English Electric Type '3's and Brush Type '2's arrived. It was at Camden until December 1965 when EMUs took over the suburban services from Euston. No. D5022 was reallocated first to Bescot, then to the Stoke and Manchester Divisions. It was renumbered as 24022 in April 1974 and was withdrawn in January 1976. Above the platforms, the large parcels depot that covered five acres is under construction.

Rebuilding 1962-1968

Once the decision was taken to electrify the West Coast Main Line, it was inevitable that the station would, at last, be completely rebuilt. The Doric Arch and Great Hall would have to be demolished, although attempts were made in vain to save the Arch and even to rebuild it nearby, but these were vetoed by the government on cost grounds. The gates from the Arch were saved and are now in the National Railway Museum and more than half of the stonework was used to fill in a channel in the River Lea in Essex. There has been a long-running campaign to extract the stones and rebuild the Arch as part of the work done for HS2.

Taylor Woodrow Construction Ltd won the contract for the work in summer 1962 and began construction of the new station while maintaining train services as far as possible, helped by the diversion of the main Manchester and West Midlands trains to St. Pancras and Paddington respectively.

English Electric Type '4' No. D235 *Apapa* after arrival in Platform 2 with an express from Liverpool Lime Street on 13th November 1962. One of the three main arrival platforms, Platform 1 on the right, is already closed for rebuilding. D235 had been named after the 1947-built Elder Dempster Lines ship, without ceremony at Crewe Works earlier in the year. The L&NWR ground signal discussed on page 16 had been removed by this date.

Brian Stephenson

Rebuilding work at Euston is well under way as English Electric Type '1' No. D8039 waits to remove a restaurant car and an Open First acting as a dining car on a gloomy 3rd March 1963. The Type '1's replaced the steam station pilots at Euston and No. D8039 had been transferred to Camden from Devons Road in March 1960. Note the contractor's bridge built right across the station which allowed them access to each platform away from the forecourt and taxi access roads. It was designed so that ramps could be added or removed as work progressed. On the left the old taxi-ramp can just be seen descending between Platforms 2 and 3, having curved all the way round outside Platform 1 from Drummond Street.

Brian Stephenson

The reconstruction work began in earnest in the Summer of 1962 and considerable demolition work was in progress on 14th June 1963. The air is full of dust as the bulldozers and cranes sweep away great swathes of the old station. Platform 6 on the right has already disappeared while the remains of Platform 7 are on the left with a board at the end directing passengers to Platforms 8 to 15.

On the same day, a closer look at the devastation on the arrivals side. Note the entrance to the Underground has not yet been swept away. One of the features of the old station were separate entrances to the 'Tube' on the platforms.

Taken just two months after the pictures on the previous page, on 28th August 1963, from the site of Platform 6 it is apparent that considerable work had already taken place on the Main Arrival platforms to the right.

On the same day, a London 'bobby' and his female colleague chat to passengers during a quiet late morning spell. This view outward on the remains of the roadway between the former Platforms 2 and 3, shows one of the old entrances to the Underground station.

Not much of the Euston Hotel remains standing in September 1963. The cars parked in front will have a coating of dust by the time they drive away!

Services had to be kept running throughout the rebuilding although many of the main line trains to Manchester and the West Midlands had been transferred to St. Pancras and Paddington. There was no alternative to the Watford electrics other than the already crowded London Transport trains. In the centre background is the stump of the Euston Hotel.

By 15th April 1965 the new station was emerging from the ruins. This view is looking outward from the barrier end of the Arrival side, on the site of former Platforms 3 on the right and 8 on the left.

EMU Driving Trailer Second No. M75151 passes under Hampstead Road Bridge on 24th March 1963. It was part of one of the three-car units built at Eastleigh for the Euston-Watford and North London electric routes in 1957/8. The design, which became Class '501' under TOPS, was similar to that of the Southern Region 'EPB', but on 57ft rather than 63ft 6in. underframes, and the droplight windows had metal safety bars due to restricted clearances in Hampstead Heath tunnel. They enabled the last of the L&NWR 'Oerlikon' stock to be taken out of service in April 1960 with the later LM&SR-built 'GEC' units lasting only a couple of years more. In 1970 the whole of the DC system was modified to operate without the negative return rail; instead the current return was made through the running rails, the 4th rail was left in place bonded to the running rails on lines shared with London Transport underground stock that still operated on that principle.

Lower right: By the end of 1965, fifteen new platforms had been completed together with a further three for parcels traffic. The approach tracks were re-organised to provide full interchangeability of routes and the 1952 signalling was replaced together with a new box which controlled the main lines out as far as South Hampstead, the Watford electric lines to Queens Park and the North London route to Primrose Hill. The first scheduled electric-hauled train from the new station was on 6th November 1965 when 'AL6' No. E3110 took out the pantograph test car and a BSK. Regular working of electric main line trains started in November 1965 and the full electric service began on 3rd January 1966.

The demolition of the Euston Hotel is almost complete as 'AL5' No. E3088 is parked at the end of Platform 9 on 30th November 1965. It was built at Doncaster in September 1962 but was not taken into stock until February 1963. It was renumbered as 85033 in June 1973 and was withdrawn in July 1984 after suffering fire damage the previous year.

Rather strangely a former L&NER horsebox is next to the 12T van in Platform 10. With its flat drop door perhaps it was being used to move equipment around because surely the new electric station would not be handling horse traffic? Note also the new 'AM10' EMU No. 058 in the background.

The rebuilding work was in two phases, firstly the trackwork and platforms, followed by the new passenger building which was not started until May 1966. It was completed in October 1968 and had a 200ft wide by 150ft deep hall under a 36ft high roof. At the front of the station between Euston Square and the station was the piazza, a large paved open area. It was intended to fund much of the rebuilding cost by building four tower office blocks and a hotel, but this was vetoed after ten years of protracted negotiations with a succession of local authorities; the three office blocks were eventually built in the late 1970s. A spacious, open concourse over two levels provided access to London Underground services, shops, restaurants and a new travel centre – the first 'one stop shop' concept where passengers could buy tickets, book sleeper and ferry services and hotel accommodation in one place. The station design specifically separated the movement of passengers and road traffic; vehicles circulated in the taxi, short stay and multi-storey car park facilities underneath the main concourse building. The only elements of the old station that were kept were the L&NWR war memorial in Euston Square, the two lodges on Euston Road and the statue of Robert Stephenson by Carlo Marochetti which was re-erected in the station piazza.

When the new Euston first opened on 14th October 1968, the spacious uncluttered frontage was considered by some observers as the late 20th century equivalent of the 1837 terminus and the concourse a worthy successor to the Great Hall. The colonnade between the piazza and the hall was 647ft long and was black and white with polished granite cladding on the rectangular columns and white mosaic horizontal facings with glass screens between them. The site it occupied was roughly that of the old station because it was constrained by the retention of Euston Square as an open space. This resulted in the platforms being on average only around 90ft nearer to the Euston Road. There were twenty platforms, five of which were for parcels and other non-passenger use, and they varied in length between 700ft and 1,300ft.

Euston in 1968

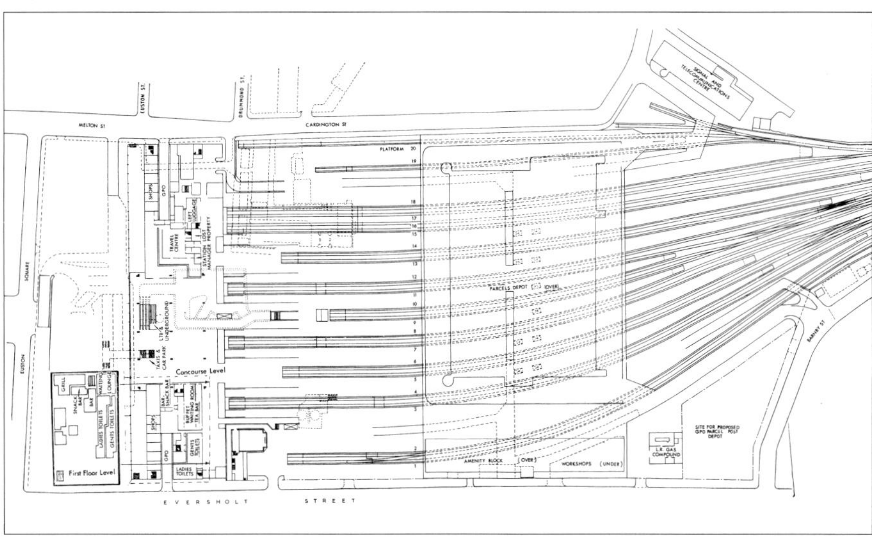

The Watford DC lines were reduced to Platforms 9 and 10; No. 11 road was used for stabling main-line electric locomotives. After arrival these followed their trains out and set back into No. 11 road; only sleeping-car and Pullman stock was initially hauled out to Stonebridge Park. Above the platforms was a very large parcels depot covering over five acres which was linked by ramps to Platforms 1, 2 and 3. Great care was taken to separate road traffic from foot traffic and all road vehicle movements within the station area were below ground.

Electrification

Electric main line services began in the week commencing 22nd November 1965 with a dozen or so trains in each direction. One of ten 'AL4's built at the North British Locomotive Company's Hyde Park Works in Glasgow as main contractor to General Electric, No. E3042, after arrival on 30th November 1965. It entered service in October 1960 and was withdrawn as No. 84007 in April 1977. The 'AL4's cost £92,365 each and were intended to have a twenty-five-year working life. As early as 1963 they were all taken out of service for urgent modification and in 1967 they were considered for withdrawal but, instead, were sent for long-term storage to the former steam shed at Bury. They were eventually refurbished at Doncaster Works in 1971/72, but were all withdrawn within a few years, the final three lasting until 1980. Latterly, they were mainly used on ECS workings between Stonebridge Park and Euston.

EMUs took over the suburban services to Northampton and Rugby, also in week commencing 22nd November. On the third day of electric operation 'AM10' No. 058 is alongside a Watford DC unit with Driving Trailer Open Brake Second No. M75166 in view. There is a marked contrast in front-end design between the dated 1950s flat front of the Watford unit and the stylish curved wrap-around of the 'AM10' although the latter still had slam doors.

The Watford DC units dated from 1957 when fifty-seven three-car sets were built at Eastleigh Works using frames supplied by Ashford Works. They were similar in style, but with a shorter underframe, to the Southern Region 'EPB' stock which used the 1951 Mk1 type all-steel body shell. Unlike the SR units the LMR specified a destination blind as well as a headcode panel.

'AL6' No. E3151 arriving with the 'Manchester Pullman' on 30th December 1966. In April 1966 the 'Manchester Pullman' had replaced the 'Midland Pullman' (operated by the diesel 'Blue Pullman' units between St. Pancras and Manchester Central) following completion of the electrification of the West Coast Main Line. The train consisted of purpose-built Mark 2 carriages in a special Pullman livery, pearl grey with blue window surrounds (a reversal of the new Inter-City livery). There were two sets of stock, one based in London and one in Manchester, each operating an outward journey in the morning and a return in the evening. There was also a less successful 'sister' 'Liverpool Pullman' service that was half Pullman (1st class) and half ordinary Mark 2 (2nd class) that ran between London Euston and Liverpool Lime Street. No. E3151 had been built by English Electric at Vulcan Foundry, and renumbered to 86212 in September 1973 after fitting with Flexicoil suspension and resilient wheels for high speed passenger operation. Fifty-two of the class were modified in this way following issues with track damage arising from the use of axle-hung traction motors rather than the bogie frame-mounted type used on the earlier electric classes.

'AL1' No. E3012 departs with a Liverpool express in the early 1970s formed of Mark 2 stock with a Mark 1 strengthener at the front. One of twenty-five of the two more successful types in the original 100 locomotives built for the first phase of the LMR electrification, the 'AL1' was built in December 1960 by Birmingham Railway Carriage & Wagon Co. at Smethwick and fitted with AEI traction motors. It was withdrawn as No. 81010 in 1990 after suffering fire damage the previous year. Full yellow ends were applied to locomotives from 1968 onwards replacing the half-panel type which had been used since 1962. The maroon Brake Second on the left rather spoils the consistency of the 'all electric railway'.

2 – Western Division sheds

Camden

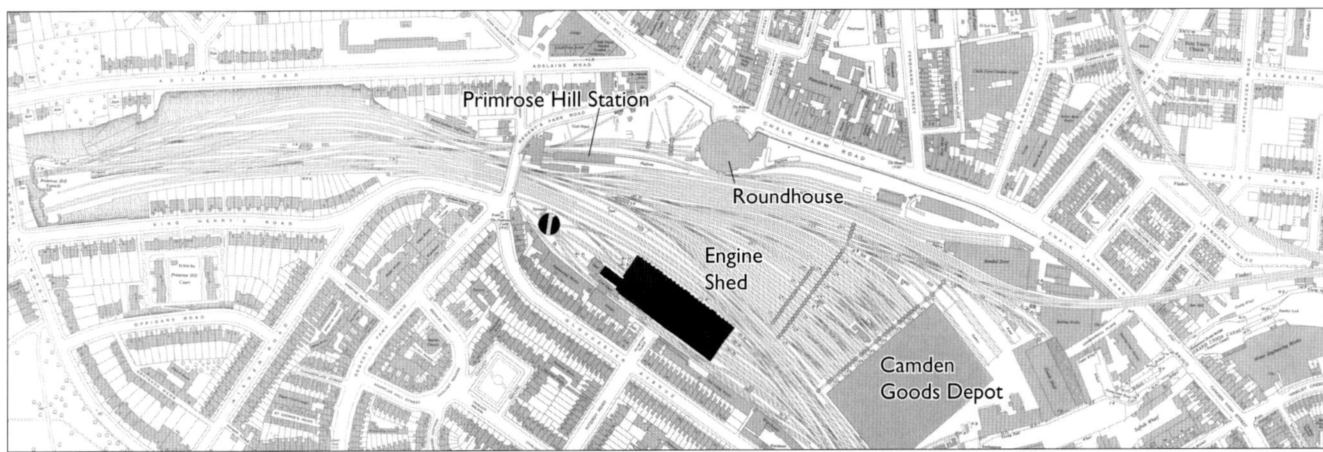

The shed was built by the L&NWR in 1847 for passenger locomotives on a cramped site at the top of Camden Bank, goods engines being housed in the 'Roundhouse' on the east side of the main line. It was improved with a mechanical coaling plant and ash-lifting plant shortly after the First World War but these were replaced with more modern facilities by the LM&SR in the mid-1930s when a 70ft turntable was installed to handle Stanier's new Pacifics. A wheel drop was installed and a machine shop added at the rear of the building since Camden was responsible for the maintenance of the express locomotives working out of Euston. As with many other London Midland Region sheds, it was partially converted for diesel traction at the end of the 1950s. Following a brief period with mixed traction, Camden's steam allocation was cleared out in September 1962 with the last few engines transferring to Willesden. Diesels had the shed to themselves for only a short time and after electrification was completed at the end of 1965, it became redundant and was closed on 3rd January 1966, although locomotives occasionally continued to stable on the site into the 1970s. Camden was coded 1B by the LM&SR and British Railways.

Right: For around four years between 1959 and 1962 the shed was host to both steam and diesel traction. An English Electric Type '4' and Type '1' take a supporting role to a gleaming crimson lake-liveried Crewe North 'Coronation' No. 46228 *Duchess of Rutland.*

'Royal Scot' No. 46115 *Scots Guardsman* on Camden's 70ft vacuum-operated turntable in 1962 and behind it, the large girder bridge carrying Regents Park Road over the main line and the goods yard throat. No. 46115 was the last of the class to be withdrawn, in January 1966, and was purchased privately for preservation. After being kept for a time on the Keighley & Worth Valley Railway it moved to the Dinting Railway Centre in 1969 where it was repaired and returned briefly to main line operation during 1979 painted in 1946 LM&SR lined black. It was not until 2008 that *Scots Guardsman* returned to the national network, working until 2017 when it was taken out of service for overhaul after the expiry of its ten-year boiler certificate.

Camden was the only shed to have every 'Coronation' Pacific allocated there at some time. Three engines, No. 46239 *City of Chester*, No. 46240 *City of Coventry* and No. 46245 *City of London*, pictured under repair on 28th April 1962, were there the longest. All three went to Camden from new and stayed until the shed closed to steam in September 1963, after which they were transferred to Willesden for around a year until their final move to Crewe North.

On the same day, No. 46234 *Duchess of Abercorn* runs out from under the coaling plant. It had been allocated to Camden from first entering service in August 1938 until March 1943, and again briefly in 1959, but went to Carlisle Upperby for its final years in service and was withdrawn in January 1963. It was one of five engines built without streamlining before the Second World War and hence does not have the utility pattern open front footplate of the engines which had previously been streamlined.

Willesden

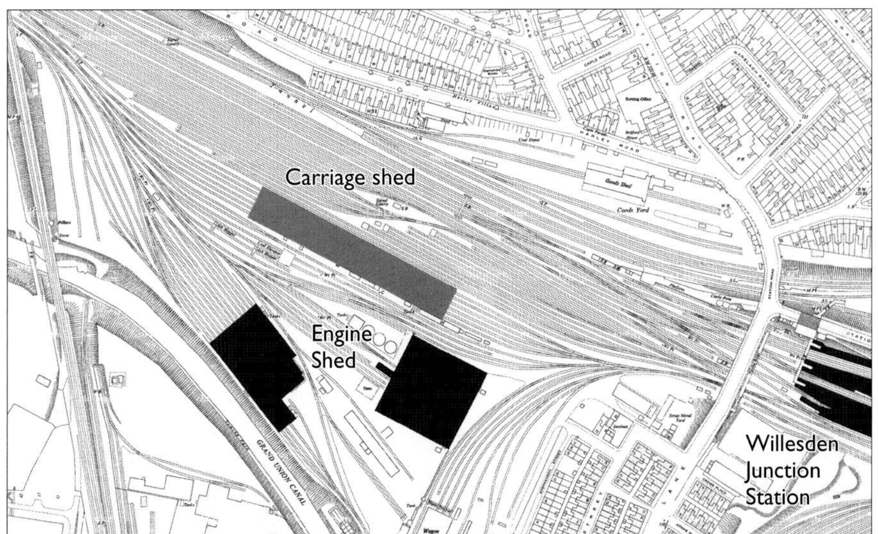

Willesden Shed was opened by the L&NWR in 1873 because the previous facility for freight engines at Camden had become outgrown. The shed also handled the work from the new carriage sidings and freight yards built at the same date. The first shed had twelve roads accommodating forty-eight engines but was enlarged in 1898 to hold sixty engines; it also had a large repair shop. As with Camden, a mechanical coaling plant and an ash lifting plant were installed in the early 1920s, and also electrical power. The LM&SR added a roundhouse to the east of the old shed in 1929 but apart from that, the shed remained virtually unchanged until the end of its days, even retaining its original roof. Willesden, which was coded 1A by the LM&SR and British Railways, was closed on 27th September 1965 and a new diesel & electric depot opened nearby; the site was used for a new Freightliner depot.

Caprotti Class '5' 4-6-0 No. 44750 in front of the ash plant on 30th April 1950. It had been built as M4750 in February 1948 and was renumbered in June 1949. No. 44750 was allocated to Longsight Shed from new until September 1960. In the background looms the massive 'centotaph' mechanical coaling plant built in the 1920s by the Mitchell Conveyor Company.

Willesden provided freight locomotives principally, but also some passenger motive power, for the London end of the West Coast Main Line. Unsurprisingly, '8F' 2-8-0s, '4F' 0-6-0s and Class '5' 4-6-0s predominate in the yard on 16th October 1955. In 1954 Willesden had 126 steam locomotives on its books: thirty-seven 2-8-0s, twenty-one 4-6-0s, ten 0-6-0s, ten 2-6-0s, ten 0-8-0s, two 2-6-4Ts, twenty-three 2-6-2Ts (mainly used for Euston empty stock workings) and thirteen 0-6-0Ts; in addition there were seventeen 0-6-0 diesel-electric shunters. The mechanical coaler is on the left out of the picture and this is the twelve-road straight shed; the roundhouse was offset to the left rear with the Grand Union Canal out of shot to the right. Behind the straight shed was a three-road heavy repair shop, accessed from the rear. The shed was closed on 27th August 1965 – three months before mainline electrification reached London.

1950s

With the Grand Union Canal on the right, 'G2A' No. 49088 is seen at its home shed in 1955. It was built by the L&NWR as Class 'G' No. 2661 and renumbered as 9088 in 1928. It was rebuilt twice by the LM&SR, firstly as a superheated 'G1' in 1933 and then as a 'G2A' with a higher pressure 175lb per sq. in. boiler, 'strengthened motion and improved brake power' in 1939. No. 49088 was withdrawn in November 1957.

Hughes-Fowler 'Crab' 2-6-0 No. 42779 at Willesden in July 1958 paired with a snap-head riveted tender that was built with Stanier 2-6-0 No. 13248, and which it ran with from February 1954. No. 42779 was at Bescot for over twenty years, from June 1937 until April 1959 when it was transferred to Aston.

1960s steam

The LM&SR put into service nearly 600 '4F' 0-6-0s based closely on the Midland Railway design, even building forty-five between 1937 and 1941 during William Stanier's tenure as CME. No. 44239 from Northampton Shed was built at Derby in April 1926 and was withdrawn in November 1963; the overhead warning plates suggest this picture dates from around 1961. The large pipe curving down from the side of the smokebox leads to the exhaust steam injector. These devices were intended to reduce coal consumption and in May 1931 the LM&SR authorised their retro-fitting to over 1,200 engines, including all of the '4F' class. However, less than 20% of these had been modified when the decision was reversed in November 1933 after the expected savings did not materialise.

Rebuilt 'Patriot' No. 45522 *Prestatyn* and 'Jubilee' No. 45721 *Impregnable* under the coaling stage on 28th April 1962. No. 45721 was at Crewe North from July 1961 until April 1964 when it went to Burton, joining twenty-five classmates, most of which had been transferred there in November 1961. No. 45522 had been rebuilt with a taper boiler in 1949; it was allocated to the LM&SR/LMR Western Division from 1935 until November 1959 when it moved to the Midland Division at Kentish Town, staying until Autumn 1961 when it was transferred to Newton Heath.

'Jubilee' No. 45698 *Mars* also on 28th April 1962 surrounded by variety of classes including a 'Britannia' 4-6-2, an '8F' 2-8-0, a Stanier 2-6-4T and a Fowler '3F' 0-6-0T. No. 45698 was allocated to Bank Hall shed at Liverpool from September 1948 until withdrawn in October 1965.

BR Standard Class '2' 2-6-2T No. 84004 from Bletchley shed, without its rear pony truck, stands in front of the Repair Shop on 17th May 1962 with English Electric Type '1' No. D8004 on the adjacent road. Willesden shed was built alongside the Paddington Branch of the Grand Union Canal, but unlike the nearby Great Western Old Oak Common shed was on the opposite bank to the footpath.

Diesels

There were two basic arrangements of LM&SR diesel-electric shunting locomotives, the jackshaft drive and the twin motor type. They could be rostered for over 6,000 hours' shunting duties per annum, and a diesel-electric when single-manned could achieve savings of around 45% compared with an equivalent steam engine and even discounting the cost of a fireman was about 18% cheaper to run. The jackshaft drive required a heavy and expensive mechanical construction and the use of connecting rods. The balance was bad, and the wheelbase had to be long enough to permit the accommodation of the jackshaft. For these and other reasons, the twin motor layout was better but when the LM&SR was first ordering the diesels in quantity in the mid-1930s the possibility of overheating when the locomotive was operating at slow speed with a heavy drawbar pull had not been overcome. It was greater than with the higher gear ratio and forced ventilation of the jackshaft type, and hence the latter were ordered as Nos 7080-7099. No. 12009 was built as LM&SR No. 7086 in November 1939 and renumbered in November 1948 with BRITISH RAILWAYS lettering on the engine compartment doors in cream Gill Sans 6in. high. It went to Willesden from Crewe South in 1945 and returned there in November 1954, by which time there were around twenty diesel shunters based there; No. 12009 was withdrawn in September 1967.

The English Electric prototype *Deltic* on shed in the late 1950s when it was working regularly on the London Midland Region between Euston and Liverpool. It is parked adjacent to the steam breakdown crane and in front of what appears to be a hand crane for use around the shed.

BTH Type '1' Bo-Bo No. D8208 at Willesden on 24th May 1959. It was built in 1958 by the Yorkshire Engine Company in Sheffield with a Paxman 800 bhp engine; Clayton (Tetbury Works) supplied the bogies and superstructure and BTH the traction motors and generator. No. D8208 was initially allocated to Devons Road, as were all the first ten of the class. It went briefly on loan to Scotland in early 1959 at Polmadie, Kittybrewster and Thornton Junction. In January 1960 No. D8208 was transferred to the Eastern Region, to Stratford, first on loan and then permanently; it was withdrawn from there in September 1968 after just ten years in service.

In the roundhouse that was built in 1929 on spare ground to the east of the existing shed, stands the second of Bulleid's diesel-electrics No. 10202 in 1961. These two Southern Railway diesels weighed 135 tons and to carry the additional weight had articulated pony trucks in a 1Co-Co1 wheel arrangement to reduce the axle loading. Although their engines were ordered from English Electric in mid-1947, construction did not begin until April 1949 and No. 10201 entered traffic over eighteen months later with No. 10202 not following until September 1951. The main differences compared with the third locomotive No. 10203 were the engines, which could only produce 1,750 bhp compared with 2,000 bhp, and the connecting gangway doors in the nose end which were dispensed with in the later locomotive. No. 10202 worked on the Southern Region until April 1955; it was transferred from Camden to Willesden in November 1959, replaced by the new English Electric Type '4's, and saw out its days on secondary work. The roundhouse had twenty-three roads arranged around a 70ft turntable, two or three of which were reserved for diesels, with DIESELS ONLY painted on the turntable well, to avoid hot cinders from steam engines igniting spilt diesel oil.

Steam and diesel locomotives used the shed at Willesden side-by-side which was not a good environment in which to operate the more sensitive modern traction. English Electric Type '4' No. D325 was the first of the final batch built at Vulcan Foundry and was delivered to Crewe North in December 1960; it was transferred to Camden in January 1961. Renumbered as No. 40125 in January 1974, it ended its days in the North West before withdrawal in June 1981. Fowler 2-6-2T No. 40049 which had been at Willesden since 1952 went to Scotland in 1959, initially on loan to Dundee Tay Bridge and then moved to Hurlford in January 1959; it returned to Willesden in August and was taken out of service in July 1961. More than a dozen of its classmates were stored there out of use by early 1958.

The Diesel and Electric Depot

Willesden Diesel and Electric Depot was built on a new site to the south of Willesden Junction station on the opposite side of the line to the old steam shed. It was sandwiched between the Watford DC lines and the main line. As was customary, there is a mix of diesel and electric traction outside the new Depot on 16th January 1966. On the left are an unidentified BR Sulzer Type '2' and an 'AL6' electric; in the centre is 'AM10' unit No. 046 and on the right are three 350bhp diesel shunters. The depot had six parallel roads each holding four locomotives inside.

Inside the depot in January 1966, 'AL5' No. E3066 on the left and 'AL2' No. E3048 on the right with an English Electric Type '4 and a DMU in the background. No. E3066 worked until July 1991, withdrawn as No. 85114 after conversion to a freight locomotive following removal of its train heating equipment; it was first renumbered as No. 85011 in October 1974. No. E3048 was taken out of service in June 1980 after fire damage. It was not formally withdrawn until June 1983 despite over £100,000 being spent on repairing it. Note the 'ground' or 'underfloor' wheel drop on the left in front of the Type '4' with its minimalistic fence protection.

Two English Electric 'AL3' Nos E3098 and E3099 outside the depot on the same day. The fifteen locomotives in the class which cost £86,704 each were one of the few unsuccessful designs from English Electric under the British Railways Modernisation Plan. These two locomotives were built in 1961 as Type 'B' Nos E3303 and E3304, geared for freight work, but were re-geared for passenger work and modified to Type 'A' and renumbered in September and November 1962 respectively. Both were later put into store, No. E3098 from April 1968 and No. E3099 from April 1969. In 1972 they were refurbished and renumbered as 83013 and 83014, but they worked again for less than a decade and went back into store before they were finally withdrawn in July 1983.

3 – Euston to Watford

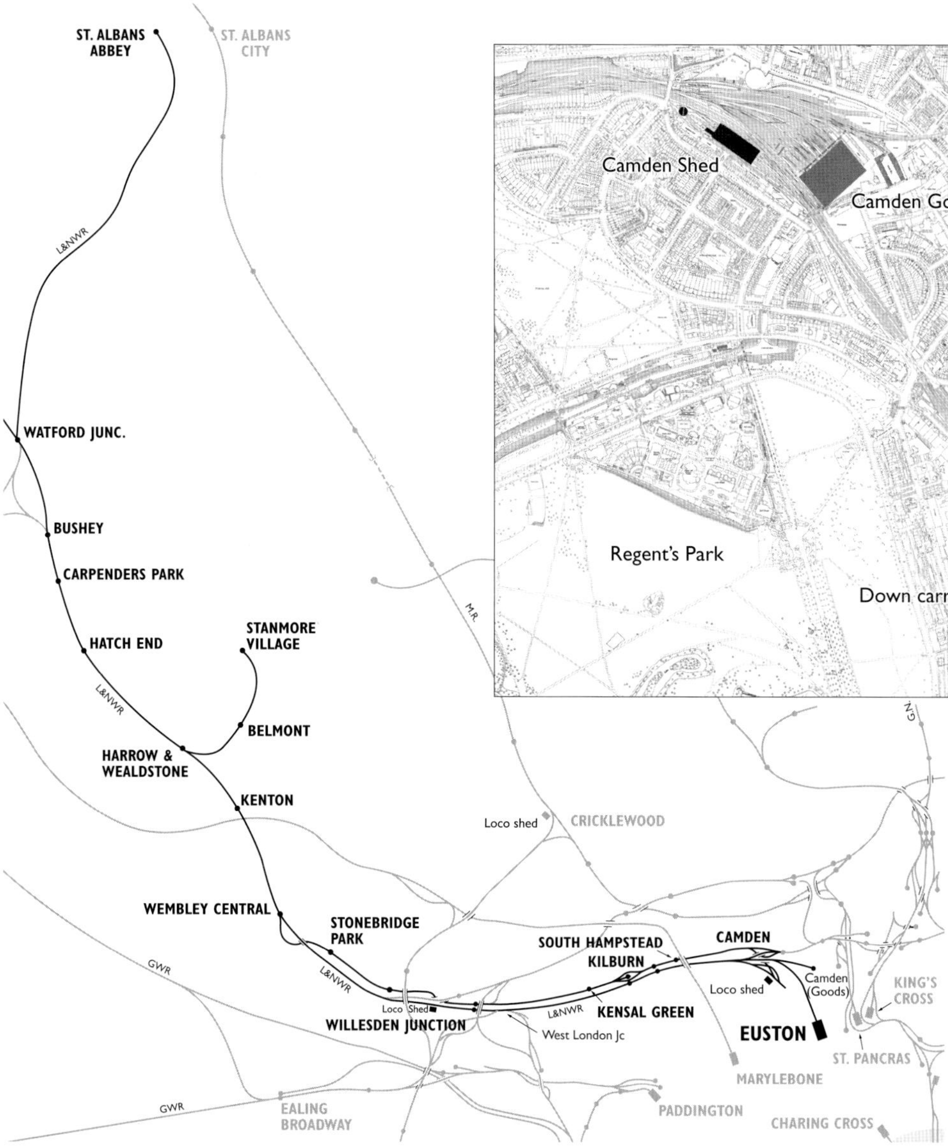

ST. ALBANS ABBEY
ST. ALBANS CITY
L&NWR
WATFORD JUNC.
BUSHEY
CARPENDERS PARK
HATCH END
STANMORE VILLAGE
BELMONT
HARROW & WEALDSTONE
KENTON
M.R.
Loco shed
CRICKLEWOOD
WEMBLEY CENTRAL
STONEBRIDGE PARK
SOUTH HAMPSTEAD
KILBURN
CAMDEN
Loco shed
Camden (Goods)
KING'S CROSS
Loco Shed
WILLESDEN JUNCTION
KENSAL GREEN
West London Jc
EUSTON
ST. PANCRAS
MARYLEBONE
GWR
EALING BROADWAY
PADDINGTON
CHARING CROSS
G.N.

Camden Road
Camden Shed
Camden Goods
Up carriage shed
Regent's Park
Down carriage shed
Euston

Euston approaches

Trains leaving Euston were faced with the 1¼ miles of Camden Bank which began at 1 in 70, easing to 1 in 112 at Euston No. 4 signal box and then after 600 yards steepened again to 1 in 77 for the final stretch up to Camden No. 1 signal box. Main line trains and a few locals were given assistance up the bank by the engine which had brought in the empty stock; these were not coupled and dropped off at the board on the south side of the canal bridge at Camden No. 1 box. The train engines of main line arrivals usually assisted the empty stock up the bank if it was being taken out to Willesden carriage sheds.

Camden

The second of the two LM&SR diesel-electrics No. 10001 climbs Camden Bank out of Euston with a Blackpool express as a 'Jubilee' arrives in 1951. It has passed Euston No. 4 signal box which became 'Euston Carriage Sidings' signal box in 1952 when the new Euston signal box was opened and took over its main line responsibility; it remained in use until September 1965 when the new power box for the electrified station came into use.

The train is crossing the bridge over the Up Engine Line and Down Empty Carriage Line which had been opened in 1906 when the approach lines had been remodelled; this allowed the carriages of arriving trains to be backed out, serviced in the West carriage yard, and then taken down to the departure platforms without affecting the main lines.

F. R. Hebron/Rail Archive Stephenson

The steep ascent of Camden Bank began immediately after leaving the platforms. 'Jubilee' No. 45688 *Polyphemus* makes its way up with the Down side carriage shed to the right off picture. It was allocated to Bushbury from July 1951 and the condition of the paintwork suggests this picture was taken soon after it received BR green livery in June 1952. There is an interesting mix of coaches; the first two are ex-LM&SR from differing periods and behind them a rake of new BR Mark 1 coaches.

Another 'Jubilee', No. 45741 *Leinster,* heads the 6.50pm express to Wolverhampton on 18th July 1953 having just passed Euston Carriage Sidings signal box. No. 45741 was the penultimate 'Jubilee' to enter service, in December 1936. It had been transferred to Bushbury for the third time, arriving from Edge Hill in June 1951, and stayed at the Wolverhampton Shed until 1959. On the right of the picture are the Down and Up Empty Carriage lines tunnelling under the main lines on their way to the Up side at Euston; beyond the box is Mornington Street Bridge. The advert on the retaining wall is for 'VOTRIX Vermouth' using the slogan 'Why pay more?'; this was a British fortified wine from Vine Products Ltd of Kingston in Surrey.

Willesden '8F' 2-8-0 No. 48325 about to pass Euston Carriage Sidings signal box as it takes empty stock from Euston up Camden Bank on 31st August 1964. It had been at the London depot since 1950 but would move away to Croes Newydd before the end of the year. The 2-8-0s were often used at this date by Willesden for ECS and parcels working at Euston. *Brian Stephenson*

BR Sulzer Type '2' Bo-Bo No. D5032 comes down Camden Bank with the 7.14am Bletchley to Euston train passing No. D5024 in the West or Up side carriage shed on 31st August 1964. Both locomotives were originally on the Eastern Region and arrived on loan to Willesden from Stratford as new Brush Type '2's were delivered there, No. D5032 at the end of 1960 and No. D5024 in March 1961; they were permanently transferred shortly afterwards. The latter was withdrawn in 1975 with fire damage but No. D5032 was saved for preservation by the T.J. Thomson scrap merchants in 1976. It was immediately loaned to the North Yorkshire Moors Railway and has worked there ever since; it was purchased by the railway in late 2016. *Brian Stephenson*

English Electric Type '1' Bo-Bo No. D8003 with the 7.30am Tring to Euston commuter service on August 31st, 1964. It had been delivered to Devons Road in August 1957 but stayed for only two years, going to Crewe South in August 1958. No. D8003 arrived in London at Willesden in October 1960 and was there until 1969. It moved around the country in its later years, to the Nottingham Division and then on to the Eastern Region and Scottish Regions, before withdrawal from Immingham in 1981 as No. 20003. *Brian Stephenson*

With the Post Office Tower in the distance, the final picture taken on 31st August 1964 shows a rare pairing of two English Electric Type '4' 1Co-Co1 diesel-electrics as Nos D293 and D213 *Andania* climb the bank past the Down side carriage shed with the 8.30am to Liverpool Lime Street. At this date the Post Office Tower was still under construction and when it opened in October 1965 it became the tallest building in the UK, at 580ft, significantly higher than the previous record holder, the 390ft high Millbank Tower. *Brian Stephenson*

Fowler '3P' 2-6-2T No. 40066 takes empty stock out of Euston on the Down Empty Carriage line, which had an incline of 1 in 50, in the 1950s. It was at Willesden from September 1952 until stored at the end of May 1959; withdrawal came in November of that year.

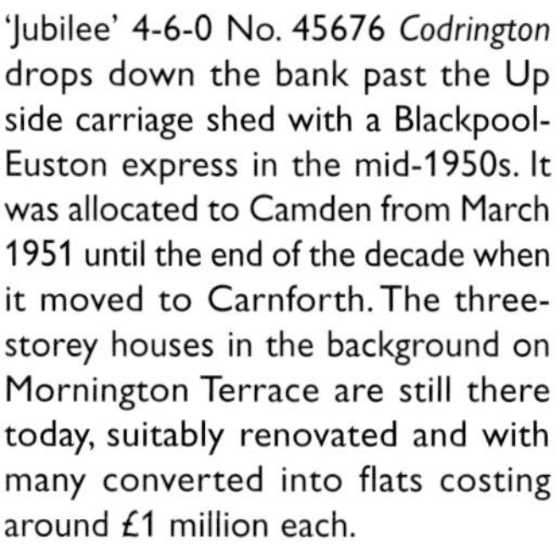

'Jubilee' 4-6-0 No. 45676 *Codrington* drops down the bank past the Up side carriage shed with a Blackpool-Euston express in the mid-1950s. It was allocated to Camden from March 1951 until the end of the decade when it moved to Carnforth. The three-storey houses in the background on Mornington Terrace are still there today, suitably renovated and with many converted into flats costing around £1 million each.

No. 46170 *British Legion* nears the top of Camden Bank, probably in 1948, given the condition of its paintwork. *British Legion* is in LM&SR 1946 lined black with the BR cab numbers and lettering applied during April 1948 in LM&SR block style; the smokebox number plate is scroll & serif, a very short-lived style which was soon replaced by Gill Sans. On the right is a '3F' 0-6-0T on the Down Empty Carriage line and on the left is the start of the goods depot.

Slightly further up the bank, Stanier 2-6-4T No. 42611 on the Down Slow with a suburban service on 19th May 1961. It had been transferred to Willesden from Bangor in September 1958 and was there until July 1965, apart from a brief return to the North Wales shed in summer 1961. The train is made up of BR Mk 1 suburban coaches and their LM&SR forerunners.

'AM10' EMU No. 048 in glistening Rail Blue set-off with cast double-arrow emblems and unpainted aluminium window frames tops Camden Bank in early 1966 with a Bletchley service. The 'AM10' units were introduced in 1965 for the electrification to Euston and were based on the Mark 2 bodyshell with curved tumblehome and wrap-around cab windows. They were the first EMUs to be fitted with disc brakes and were also the first with air-cooled rectifiers, inductors and transformers, and to have the new all-blue livery. They worked on Euston to Bletchley, Northampton and Birmingham services until 1988 when they were replaced by Class '317' units; the now Class '310's were transferred to the LT&SR line and the last sets were taken out of service in 2002.

On the same day, 'AL6' No. E3141 on a Manchester express with a train of the blue and grey Mark 2 coaches built for the new electric service; the effect of the new stock was spoilt by the Mark 1 buffet cars which were included in the new sets. No. E3141 was one of sixty built at Vulcan Foundry but originally planned for Doncaster, it entered traffic in February 1966. It was renumbered as 86208 when modified with Flexicoil suspension and resilient wheels for higher speed passenger operation in July 1973. It was withdrawn in October 2002 after spending the previous eighteen months in store.

Compound 4-4-0 No. 41152 in immaculate British Railways lined black livery heads north with a short parcels train on 3rd June 1950. It was built for the LM&SR by the North British Locomotive Company in 1925 and had been a long-time Rugby engine since before the war, although it would depart to Brunswick, the former Cheshire Lines Committee shed at Liverpool, in January 1951. No. 41152 is passing the 'LMS Camden Goods Station' which somewhat boldly offered 'One day transits to & from all important towns'. The train is an interesting mix of old parcels stock with a Southern Railway parcels van at the front, two ex-L&NWR bogie vans separated by a LM&SR six-wheeled fish or milk van, and what appears to be a Stanier Brake Third bringing up the rear – no doubt the guard had chosen to ride in this!

LM&SR diesels Nos 10001 and 10000 pass Camden Goods Depot as they come down Camden Bank with the up 'Royal Scot' from Glasgow Central to Euston in 1951. In the background beyond the depot yard is the Camden Roundhouse, the original London & Birmingham Railway goods engine shed built in 1846 which was 157ft in diameter with the conical shaped roof supported on twenty-four Doric columns. Within around ten years it was superseded because it was unable to accommodate the longer engines and tenders which had come into use. Since then it has had a variety of uses including a half-century as a bonded warehouse for the gin distillers W. & A. Gilbey Ltd. In 1964 a scheme began to transform it into an arts venue, and it re-opened for this purpose in October 1966, hosting famous 1960s pop stars such as Jimi Hendrix, The Doors and Jefferson Airplane. It fell into disuse in the early 1990s and was eventually restored in 2006 and is still in use today. *F.R. Hebron/Rail Archive Stephenson*

Stanier Class '5' 4-6-0 No. 45064 with a Down express passing Camden Shed on 17th June 1952. It was the penultimate engine in the first batch of the class built at Vulcan Foundry in 1934 and was allocated to Willesden from June 1948 until May 1960 when it moved away to Bescot. The roof of the Goods Depot is visible in the distance and on the left is Camden No. 2 signal box which controlled the North London line to Chalk Farm/Primrose Hill Station and the tracks into Camden Goods Yard. The coaches, except for the full brake at the front, are all in 'blood and custard' livery at this relatively early date after this style was adopted by British Railways at the beginning of 1949.

Two LM&SR built Euston-Watford three-car EMUs pass Camden with a Watford to Euston service on 1st February 1959. The Driving Motor Third coach is at the front. Note on the right the insulated meat container and the Lowflat carrying a Singer Gazelle car, a more luxurious version of the more common Hillman Minx. *K.L. Cook/Rail Archive Stephenson*

South Hampstead

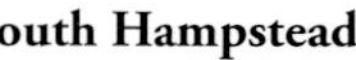

BR Sulzer Type '2' No. D5002 emerges from Primrose Hill Tunnel and approaches South Hampstead Station with a Down 'ordinary passenger train' on 31st May 1962. It was built at Derby Works, entering service in December 1958, and almost immediately went on loan to the Southern Region pending the arrival of its BRC&W Type '3's and the completion of the North Kent electrification scheme; in all the London Midland Region loaned fifteen of its new Type '2's. Five of these, including No. D5002, had their steam heating boilers and boiler water tanks removed to reduce their weight and improve their route availability. No. D5002 did not return to the London Midland until 19th May 1962 and although allocated to Crewe South went immediately on loan to Willesden for a month. As a souvenir from its days on the Southern it has additional lamp irons below the horizontal handrails to carry the SR headcode discs. No. D5002 was renumbered in April 1974 as No. 24002 and after moving around the London Midland Region ended its days in Scotland and was withdrawn from Eastfield in October 1975. South Hampstead Station was opened by the L&NWR in 1879 as Loudoun Road, closed in 1917 and re-opened as South Hampstead in July 1922; it is still in use today as part of the 'London Overground'.

Kilburn

Fowler 2-6-4T No. 42422 rushes through Kilburn High Road with a Down local on 9th June 1960. It was one of the last three engines in the class, entering service in December 1933, almost two years after William Stanier took over as the LM&SR Chief Mechanical Engineer, and incorporating a number of changes such as a new design of bogie, no bogie brakes, plain section coupling rods, snap-head riveting and the so-called 'limousine' cabs. These had side windows and full height doors instead of the large cut-outs either side of the gangway, which had proved unacceptable when operating bunker-first because the incoming air blew coal around the cab making conditions extremely bad for the crew. No. 42422 arrived at Willesden from Southport in September 1959, its second spell at the shed, but was transferred to Northwich soon after this picture was taken, at the end of July. It was fitted with new cylinders and outside steam pipes in January 1954.

More action on 9th June 1960 as the Down 'Mancunian' passes through behind Camden-allocated 'Royal Scot' No. 46146 *The Rifle Brigade*; its original name was *Jenny Lind* until 1936. The workshop sign above the engine's smokebox reads 'J. R. Bright Coach Painting', reminding us of the wonderful diverse nature of businesses in the area. One wonders if he had to stop delicate work when an express passed by?

Just over a year later, Stanier Class '5' 4-6-0 No. 45027 passes Kilburn High Road Station with a northbound express on 23rd June 1961. It had been allocated to Willesden since the end of the war but would leave for Mold Junction in June 1962. No. 45027 was one of the first few Vulcan Foundry-built engines and was fitted with a sloping throatplate, domed boiler in December 1936. Mr Bright appears to still be in business, but his advertising sign looks very tatty and does nothing to promote it.

Kensal Green

'3F' 0-6-0T No. 47483 has just emerged from Kensal Green Tunnel with Empty Coaching Stock Stock, almost certainly for Willesden carriage sidings, on 10th September 1960. The tank was transferred to Willesden from Devons Road when that shed closed to steam in 1958 and it moved to Lancaster Green Ayre in November 1960. *K.L. Cook/Rail Archive Stephenson*

BR '9F' 2-10-0 No. 92160 with an Up freight nearing Kensal Green Tunnel on 9th September 1961. It is hard to believe that No. 92160 was less than four years old when this picture was taken, and it would be withdrawn in less than seven years' time. It was originally allocated to Wellingborough and moved to Kettering in September 1958. This is an interesting working; the train is made up of tube wagons and bogie bolsters carrying long pipes, but as this is south of Willesden it must either be heading for Camden goods yard, which mainly handled perishable van traffic, or for the North London lines at Camden – an unusual route as it would have been expected to turn off at Willesden Junction. *K.L. Cook/Rail Archive Stephenson*

Willesden Junction

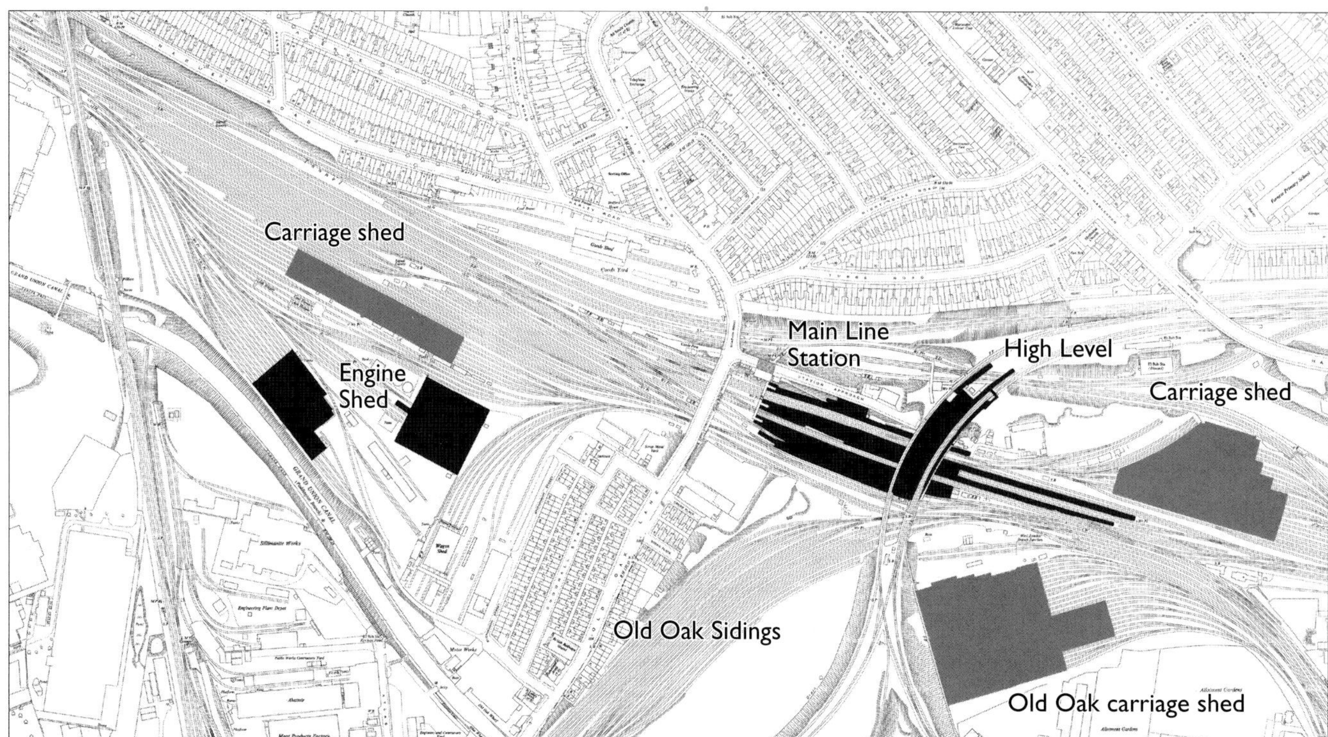

The two stations at Willesden Junction are on the right with the High Level tracks of the North London line crossing over the Low Level main line station before dividing, with the fork to the right going to the West London line to Kensington (Olympia) and Clapham Junction and the left to Acton, Kew and Richmond. On the left are the engine shed, the extensive freight sidings and carriage shed and at the bottom right part of the Great Western Old Oak Common complex.

Fowler '3P' 2-6-2T No. 40007 takes Empty Coaching Stock for the 'Caledonian' to Euston in July 1959. It had been at Willesden since January 1951 and left in August 1960, moving to Widnes for its final year in service.

Pacifics

The heyday of the 'Princess Royal' Pacifics was in the immediate pre-war years and they never regained their pre-eminent position once the 'Coronations' were introduced. After nationalisation, they continued to work heavily loaded front-line expresses, particularly on the London-Liverpool trains such as 'The Shamrock' and 'The Red Rose'. No. 46208 *Princess Helena Victoria* was one of four of the class to be repainted from green into crimson lake livery; this was done during a Light Intermediate overhaul which began shortly after this picture was taken at Willesden Junction when it was working 'The Shamrock' from Liverpool in early August 1958.

No. 46228 *Duchess of Rutland* is nearing the end of its journey with the Up 'Royal Scot' in late 1959 or 1960. The 'Coronation's themselves would soon be displaced from their front-line express work as English Electric Type '4' diesels took over. *Duchess of Rutland* was repainted in crimson lake with LM&SR-style lining during a 'Heavy Intermediate' repair completed in June 1958 and AWS was fitted in September 1959.

Southern interlopers

'Lord Nelson' No. 30851 *Sir Francis Drake* after taking over an excursion from a London Midland engine at Willesden in May 1959. It will work back to the Southern Region over the West London line through Kensington Olympia to Clapham Junction. Allocated to Eastleigh from January 1949 until withdrawal in December 1961, No. 30851 was one of two 'Nelson's to retain the 'piano front' as a throwback to when it was fitted with new cylinders in 1939 that had 8in. piston valves instead of the 10in. size on the rest of the class.

It is a Summer Saturday, 25th August 1962, at Willesden Junction looking south towards Euston, with the curve onto the West London Line on the right. Over to the left of No. 3 signal box the 'Jubilee' 4-6-0 in the platform has brought in the 10.57am Walsall - Hastings which will turn south on to the West London line. In the opposite direction, the 10.45am Hastings - Wolverhampton High Level will have come via Brighton (reversing there) and Clapham Junction, and is approaching headed by Bulleid 'West Country' Pacific No. 34101 *Hartland*. Both trains will change locomotives in the station, the Southern Region engine handing over to a London Midland one and vice versa.

Passenger tanks

Fairburn 2-6-4T No. 42099 passing through Willesden Junction (Low Level) with empty stock for Euston on 25th August 1962; three of the first four are ex-L&NER Gresley coaches. No. 42099 was built at Brighton in August 1950 and was originally on the Southern Region, moving to Watford in December 1959 and then to Willesden in June 1962.

Fairburn 2-6-4T No. 42234 waits in the platform while working empty stock from Euston on 29th September 1962. No. 42234 was a Derby built engine for the London Midland Region and it was at Willesden from December 1957 until withdrawn in February 1964. In the background behind the engine Willesden High Level station is just visible straddling the main line platforms. The 'New' station, on the electrified Euston/Broad Street - Watford Junction lines, which was shared with London Transport Bakerloo Line trains, is over to the left. The main line platforms were closed on 3rd December 1962, before the West Coast Main Line was electrified.

Tender-first Stanier Class '5' 4-6-0 No. 44679 shunts across the Paddington Branch of the Grand Union Canal at Willesden South West Sidings, also known as Old Oak Sidings, on the West London line in the early 1960s, after the fitting of AWS in October 1961. It was allocated to Crewe North from new in August 1950 until the shed closed in May 1965. Acton Lane Power Station cooling towers are in the background. Note the former Southern Railway brake van at the front of the train.

Birmingham Railway Carriage & Wagon Co. Type '3' Bo-Bo No. D6509 gets the road from Willesden Junction No. 3 signal box with a freight train for the Southern Region over the West London line on 13th November 1962. No. D6509 was built in May 1960 and became No. 33009 in March 1974; it was named *Walrus* in September 1991 but ironically was withdrawn after an accident while working a train of ballast hoppers out of Meldon Quarry in December 1991. The first wagon is a ply-sided sliding door LM&SR wartime-built van which is carrying ICI fertiliser if the label is to be believed.

Brian Stephenson

The massive bright yellow painted 72ft high Arrol travelling gantry cranes tower over Willesden Freightliner Terminal in June 1971. The cranes which each weighed between 200 and 300 tons were removed in February 2019 to make way for a logistics hub to support HS2 construction. The terminal was built on the site of the steam depot which closed in September 1965.

Stonebridge Park

Stonebridge Park Depot which was built by the L&NWR to maintain the Watford electric units still had its World War Two camouflage in place in the 1960s. On the left is one of the original L&NWR 'Oerlikon' sets – probably the unit noted in December 1960 as retained for shunting at the depot, working until October 1963, eight months after the remainder had been taken out of passenger service. The motor car from this set has been preserved as part of the National Collection. In the background is the L&NWR-built power station which supplied electricity for the Watford units.

'4F' 0-6-0 No. 44116 with a train of 40-ton coal hoppers unloading at Stonebridge Park power station on 2nd May 1953. It had been allocated to Willesden since the mid-1940s; presumably it had taken over from the train engine, probably an '8F', which had brought the train south from Shipley Colliery near Nottingham via Leicester, Market Harborough and Northampton to the L&NWR-built generating station which provided power for the Watford electrics. Thirty 40-ton bogie hopper wagons were built for the working by the Birmingham Railway Carriage & Wagon Company in 1929 to LM&SR diagram D1708 as lot No. 457 and were numbered 189301-189330. The trains ran until the closure of the power station in 1967. *C.R.L. Coles/Rail Archive Stephenson*

Wembley Central

Class '5' 4-6-0 No. 45348 and an unidentified classmate at Wembley Central with the 11.5am Liverpool-Euston on Saturday 16th August 1958. No. 45348 was a long-term Carlisle Upperby engine, from August 1941 until October 1958 when it moved to Crewe North. The Ruston shovel excavator crane, owned by Greenham contractors, appears to be ready for a serious PW possession, and has already been positioned between the running tracks off its Lowmac. Note the old sleepers to protect the track as it was moved sideways off the rail vehicle. A temporary electric light has been erected and there is a line of pipes laid out along the wooden platform. It will probably be used to dig a trench between the running lines for these to be fitted over the forthcoming night and following Sunday.

When there was a football match at the nearby stadium, Wembley Central would see a stream of specials arriving from all parts of the country. This was the occasion of the FA Cup Final on 5th May 1962 in which Tottenham Hotspur beat Burnley 3-1. 'Jubilee' 4-6-0 No. 45704 *Leviathan*, which has brought in a train carrying Burnley supporters, was at Rugby from January 1961 until June 1963.

Another special arrives at Wembley Central on the same day, this time from Euston, headed by Stanier 2-6-4T No. 42470 from Willesden.

South Kenton

A BR-built Watford EMU departs to Euston from South Kenton on 30th May 1966. There were no platforms on the main lines, only on the electric lines which were shared with the London Transport trains until 1982. The code '81' signifies a Down train so only the destination indicator has been changed.

Driving Trailer Open Brake Second No. M75182M is leading as the EMU passes Northwick Park on the left as it approaches South Kenton from Watford on 1st May 1966. It is in the later lined green livery carried by some of the sets. The London Transport Metropolitan route crossed over the lines in the distance and its Northwick Park Station is just off scene to the right.

The first of the short-lived North British built 'AL2' electrics No. E3046 at South Kenton with a train to Carlisle on 30th May 1966. Already the electric is showing signs of wear – some of the grilles are falling out. No. E3046 was in service only from September 1960 until January 1971 when it caught fire while working a Euston-Manchester express and was immediately withdrawn.

South Kenton to Harrow

With the Watford electric lines on the right, Stanier 2-6-4T No. 42585 produces a good display of smoke for the camera as it heads a Euston-Watford commuter train between Harrow and Kenton on 21st August 1962. The Class '4' tank was at Willesden from February 1959 until withdrawn in November 1962.

Stanier Class '5' 4-6-0 No. 45494 from Crewe South heads a long southbound parcels train on 21st August 1962. It was built at Derby in January 1944, one of the first batch of the class built during the Second World War. The two leading vehicles are LM&SR slab-sided 42ft CCTs; there was a pair of these off the running tracks stranded at the throat of Euston in the early 1970s for use as stores.

'Britannia' 4-6-2 No. 70045 *Lord Rowallan* between Harrow and Kenton with the Up 'Lakes Express' on 22nd August 1962. It was always on the London Midland Region, originally at Holyhead for the 'Irish Mail', but had moved to Aston in July 1962 although it returned to Holyhead at the end of the year. It had a high capacity BR1D tender that carried nine tons of coal and 4,725 gallons of water compared with seven tons and 4,250 gallons for the early 'Britannia's.

Harrow & Wealdstone

LM&SR-built diesel-electric No. 10000 on a northbound Class '4' fitted freight approaching Headstone Lane in 1952. The large BR emblem was applied during a 'Heavy General' repair completed in March 1951, replacing the cast LMS lettering which it had when new in December 1947. In 1953 British Railways decided to concentrate all the prototype main line diesels on the Southern Region and No. 10000 went to Nine Elms in March. A London Transport Bakerloo Line tube train is on the extreme right of the picture.

The two LM&SR diesels worked both passenger and freight duties while on the London Midland Region in the early 1950s. When operating singly, Nos 10000 and 10001 were employed mostly on Euston to Crewe, Liverpool or Blackpool trains, although often loaded to 450 tons or more. No. 10000 passes through Harrow & Wealdstone with the Down 'Manxman' to Liverpool in 1952, a train usually worked by a 'Princess Royal' 4-6-2. Harrow No. 2 signal box on the right was a L&NWR 1904 design built in 1923 when reversing sidings were provided for the introduction of the Watford EMUs on the 'New Line'; it was closed in 1988. The dreadful multiple collision on 8th October 1952 occurred just where No. 10000 was photographed.

No-one on the platform is paying attention to 'Coronation' Pacific No. 46229 *Duchess of Hamilton* as it rushes through Harrow & Wealdstone with the southbound 'Caledonian' in 1957, its first year of operation. The load was restricted to eight coaches weighing 280 tons tare allowing a 6 hr 40 min schedule between London and Glasgow with a two-minute stop at Carlisle. The timing was similar to that of the pre-war 'Coronation Scot', taking only ten minutes longer despite the considerably more difficult post-war operating environment, and the lightweight train made it an easy task for a 'Coronation'. The London Underground train of 1938 stock on the left is on the Bakerloo Line to Watford which was cut-back to terminate at Harrow from 1982 onwards. No. 46229 was saved for preservation by the Butlin's Holiday Camp company and in 1975 became part of the National Collection. It was restored to operational condition in 1980 and worked on the main line until 1985. In 2009 after several years of work it was refitted with a streamline casing which it had last had in 1947 and is currently on static display at the National Railway Museum at York.

Stanier Class '5' 4-6-0 No. 45493 In front of Harrow No. 1 signal box which controlled the main lines as it sets off with a northbound train on 24th August 1958. It was one of those built at Derby and was allocated to Rugby between October 1949 and June 1963. The leading coach is an LM&SR Period 1 Brake Composite No. SC6632M, the number indicating it was allocated to the Scottish Region for maintenance and accounting purposes.

Stanier 2-6-0 No. 42975 from Aston with a southbound Class 'H' unfitted freight with a former banana van leading at Harrow on 11th September 1959. In common with the rest of the class, it had moved around numerous times, mostly to former L&NWR sheds, and only stayed at the Birmingham shed until September 1960. Although maintained at Horwich Works, none were allocated to the Central Division, perhaps because the ex-L&YR preferred its 'own' Hughes-Fowler 'Crabs'. The Stanier engines were mainly employed on freight work although they did some secondary passenger work and were used on summer excursions.

Two of the original L&NWR 'Oerlikon' sets on a service to Broad Street have just left Harrow & Wealdstone station which is visible beyond the bridge on 11th November 1959. This was their last full year in service and all had gone within six months of this picture. The leading vehicle is M28284 which was a Motor Open Brake Second with forty-eight seats and fitted with four 240hp Oerlikon Traction Motors. Thirty-eight of these three-car units were built in 1916, the motor cars coming from the Metropolitan Carriage, Wagon & Finance Company in Birmingham and the trailers from the L&NWR Wolverton Works. A further thirty three-car sets were ordered in 1921 for the completion of Watford 'New Line' electrification.

An interesting working of a MR Johnson '3F' 0-6-0 which has just passed under the imaginatively titled 'The Bridge' with a southbound freight on 22nd August 1959. No. 43325, which was built by Kitson in 1892, was transferred to Watford from Longsight in July 1958 having been previously at Canklow and Grimesthorpe; it was withdrawn in February 1961. In the background on the right Pickford's Depository is just visible above the trees. The Pickfords firm was part of the Hays Wharf Cartage company which was nationalised in 1945 and as BRS (Pickfords) Ltd became part of the National Freight Consortium which was privatised in 1982.

Ivatt Class '2' 2-6-2T No. 41223 was working a seven-coach northbound local at Harrow & Wealdstone Station on 10th May 1960. This was during the period it was allocated to Watford, between June 1958 and December 1962.

A northbound Class '7' freight headed by a 'G2A' 0-8-0 runs through Harrow & Wealdstone on 22nd August 1960. No. 49314 was built by the L&NWR in 1918 as a 'G1' 0-8-0 and modified to a 'G2A' in 1947 with a new higher pressure boiler, strengthened motion and improved brake power. It was allocated to Nuneaton from March 1955 until May 1962, moving to Wigan Springs Branch. Note how by this date the wooden ex-Private Owner wagons have been superceded by steel 16T mineral wagons.

The Stanmore Branch

The short, two miles-long Stanmore Branch was connected to the main line by a north-facing junction and hence direct commuter services could not run to or from London, restricting its operation to a shuttle service from Harrow. The LM&SR built a new intermediate single platform halt at Belmont in 1932, but passenger numbers were healthy enough to justify a complete rebuild of the station with improved facilities by 1937. The branch beyond Belmont, including Stanmore Village Station was closed on 15th September 1952 but the passenger and goods service to Belmont continued until 1964. The prototype Associated Commercial Vehicles (ACV) diesel four-wheeled railbus ran trials in September 1954 and briefly appeared on the line again in 1955. One of the later ACV units returned in August 1957 but only worked until April 1958 and sporadically thereafter before the units were taken out of service in 1960; they were replaced by Cravens two-car multiple units.

Watford's motor-fitted Ivatt Class '2' 2-6-2T No. 41220 worked on both the Watford-St. Albans service and the Stanmore branch. No. 41220 was propelling the shuttle service to Stanmore at Belmont on 4th November 1950. Built at Crewe in September 1948, and after running-in at Crewe North it was allocated to Watford until April 1958, although it had several short loan spells away during 1957. The engine was always at the Harrow end of the two-coach push-pull set.

No. 41220 pauses at Belmont on its way back to Harrow. The passenger service on the branch was cut back in September 1952 from Stanmore to Belmont, reducing the journey time from seven to four minutes. The station was only opened in 1932, almost fifty years after the line itself, to serve a rapidly growing suburb. The station building dated from 1937, replacing the original timber halt on the site. Note the Midland Railway-designed signal box built directly on to the platform.

The Stanmore push-pull service was also worked by auto-fitted Fowler 2-6-2Ts from Watford. One of the regulars was No. 40020 which was at Stanmore Village on 5th August 1952, the month before the station was closed. No. 40020 was allocated to Watford until June 1958, except for two months at Warwick in mid-1956. The overgrown track on the left was formerly the run-round loop until push-pull operation was introduced and was latterly used to store rolling stock.

On the same day, Stanmore Village station was deserted at 7pm in the evening. From the entrance it looked more like a small country church than a railway station with its entrance through a buttressed portico and the square tower had an ornamental spire. The red brick construction had dressed freestone embellishments and was built in this style to appease the local Parish Council who were unhappy with the intrusion of the railway in 1889. The 'Village' suffix was added in 1950 to avoid confusion with London Transport's Bakerloo Line Stanmore Station. After the passenger service ended in 1952, the goods service continued and the line was not finally closed until July 1964.

Hatch End

Viewed from the cattle bridge north of Hatch End, 'Jubilee' No. 45635 *Tobago* heads a Relief to Manchester on the Down Fast on 13th July 1957. No. 45635 was on Newton Heath's books from 1943 until 1964 and would not normally be seen in the Capital.

On the same day, Coronation No. 46240 *City of Coventry* with a seventeen-coach Up express, north of Hatch End near Oxhey Lane Bridge. It was built in 1940 and allocated to Camden until the shed closed to steam in September 1963 when it was transferred to Willesden for around a year before its final move to Crewe North. It worked the final steam-hauled service to depart from Euston on 29th August 1964, 'The Lakes Express' as far as Crewe. The coaches all appear to be old LM&SR-built stock; several are wooden bodied from the 1920s and are in a mix of 'Blood and Custard' and maroon liveries. The first two are probably strengtheners since the third vehicle is a Brake Third and would normally head the train.

Carpenders Park

Carpenders Park Station is situated just south of Bushey and Oxhey Station on the Watford electric or 'New Lines'. The first station was opened by the London & North Western Railway on 1st April 1914 only to close on 1st January 1917. The original station was built primarily to serve the nearby golf course. It was situated 230 yards further north than the current site and was a wooden two platform structure with a linking footbridge. It reopened on 5th May 1919, served initially only by London Electric Railway (later London Underground) trains but L&NWR electric trains were reinstated from 10th July 1922. The original station closed on 17th November 1952 when the present station opened. For our intrepid photographer it was an island platform ideally situated to the east of the main Fast lines with the Slow lines, used primarily for freight, beyond. It is a straight section of the line with good views south towards Euston at the end of an eight mile climb from Willesden at a grade of 1 in 339. The line then levels through the station and beyond, curving into the cutting leading to Bushey Troughs. All of the pictures here were taken on the same day, Monday 29th August 1960.

Stanier Class '5' No. 45191 at Carpenders Park on a Down parcels. It was allocated to Northampton from January 1945 until two weeks after this picture was taken when it moved to Rugby. The short train is an eclectic mix of vehicles with a Southern Railway-designed 12 ton van at the front, followed by a GWR Collett full Brake, a BR Mark 1 full Brake, a LM&SR 50ft full Brake and what appears to be a LM&SR passenger vehicle downgraded to parcels use trailing at the rear.

Willesden 'Jubilee' 4-6-0 No. 45722 *Defence* is working hard as it reaches the end of the eight miles long, 1 in 339 climb from Willesden, with a Down class 'C' express freight. There are a large number of empty meat containers at the front of the train, probably bound for either Holyhead or Scotland and a return cargo. Note the unique colour light signal devised by the LM&SR Signal Engineer A.F. Bound as used on the Watford electric lines and installed in 1932/3. Each signal's aspect was automatically returned to red on the passage of a train. The actual signal is the top aspect displaying either red or green, the two below are a marker light and a repeater.

'Princess Royal' 4-6-2 No. 46203 *Princess Margaret Rose* heads south with a thirteen-coach express. The fourth vehicle is a Brake Third so the previous three coaches (including the leading Brake Third) may be a separate portion, possibly from Windermere. No. 46203 was on loan to Camden from Edge Hill for three weeks from 20th August, and still has an 8A shedplate. Perhaps Camden knew the allocation was temporary and had better things for their fitters to do than to change its plate. After withdrawal in October 1962, No. 46203 was purchased for display at Butlin's Holiday Camp in Pwllheli and remained there until 1975. It moved to the Midland Railway Centre at Butterley and was restored to operational condition, working on the main line between 1990 and 1996.

A Euston-bound EMU calls at the 1952-built station as an unidentified '8F' 2-8-0 takes a train of empties northwards. It would be nice to think our photographer has just arrived on this service from Watford but as this scene would be repeated all day it could have been anytime during his visit. The second empty mineral wagon is interesting as it has cupboard type doors which, like the 'French' 16T mineral wagons, would foul the adjoining line if they became open.

It would not be long before the southern end of the West Coast Main Line would be dominated by the English Electric diesels and scenes like this became commonplace. It is often forgotten that the first ten of the class delivered in 1958 were all allocated to the Eastern Region and only from No. D210 onwards, commencing in May 1959, did the London Midland Region start to receive their allocation. However, by the end of August 1960 the LMR would have thirty-four of the class. No. D224 passes an unidentified classmate on a Down express with a LM&SR Period 1 Brake Third of 1920s vintage at the front, but still in good condition with its beading intact. In August 1962 No. D224 became one of the twenty-five members of the class to be named, becoming *Lucania* at Crewe Works, the plates being fixed without a naming ceremony.

The Southern Railway Bulleid-designed diesel-electrics ended their days on outer suburban Rugby or Northampton stopping or 'ordinary passenger' trains. This one is made up of a motley collection of mainly ex-LM&SR non-corridor stock. No. 10202 was in service until November 1962 and was then stored at Derby until officially withdrawn in December 1963. The three members of the class were left on the scrap line at Derby Works, becoming increasingly decrepit, until eventually they were scrapped at Cashmore's, Great Bridge in 1968.

Bushey

'Jubilee' No. 45721 *Impregnable* with a heavy Down express at Bushey on 26th April 1948. It is in BR lined black livery with an 'Old Standard' 3,500 gallon tender; when built in 1936 it was paired with a second-hand tender from a 'Royal Scot' and kept this until 1962. No. 45721 was at Willesden from June 1947 until May 1949 when it returned to Bushbury.

Crewe North 'Royal Scot' No. 46161 *King's Own* working an Up express on 25th March 1953. It had been rebuilt with a taper boiler in 1946. Note the Watford electric lines on the left and the conical water tower for the water troughs on the right.

Another picture on 25th March 1953 was taken from a lower angle to frame Longsight 'Jubilee' No. 45740 *Munster* on a southbound express. It had been at the Manchester shed since 1943 but would move to Camden within three months of this picture. No. 45740 had been paired from new with 3,500 gallon tender No. 3926 which had been built with 'Royal Scot' No. 6130, and kept this until withdrawn in October 1963. With almost 200 engines in the class, the 'Jubilee's were by far the most numerous ex-LM&SR express engines and dominated both the Western and Midland Division passenger services with the rebuilt '7P' 4-6-0s and Pacifics only used on the heaviest or fastest trains.

'Princess Royal' 4-6-2 No. 46208 *Princess Helena Victoria* picks-up water at Bushey troughs with the Down 'Red Rose' to Liverpool on 3rd May 1958. It was allocated to Edge Hill from September 1951 until withdrawal in 1962 and was a regular on the London to Liverpool expresses.

The electric lines have turned off at Bushey & Oxhey Station for their diversion to Watford High Street thereby leaving just the four main line tracks. Stanier '8F' 2-8-0 No. 48074 is between Bushey and Watford Junction with a long train of northbound empties in the late 1950s, with a high proportion of steel opens in this late view, including a 'French' cupboard door mineral wagon leading the rake. The '8F' was one of sixty-nine of the class purchased by the LM&SR from Vulcan Foundry as part of the mid-1930s 'Scrap and Build' policy supported by government guaranteed loans at low rates of interest; it was at Willesden from June 1951 until July 1959.

Watford Junction

This three-car, four-wheel demonstration railbus unit was built by British United Traction in May 1952 using bodywork assembled by Park Royal and powered by the company's own AEC engines, of the type used in London's buses. The unit is seen at Watford Junction soon after it began two weeks of trial running on the Watford-St. Albans Abbey line in July 1952. It had side valances and droplight windows, unlike the similar sets bought by BR in 1955, and was finished in a two-tone grey livery with red lining. With its bus origins, it bore a striking resemblance to the much-maligned British Rail 'Pacers' introduced thirty years later, and with commendable foresight the *Railway Observer* commented *'The acceleration with a small passenger load was very good, as was the riding on good track. The effect of bad joints, however, on part of the branch was very noticeable and made the riding rather uncomfortable. It remains to be seen whether the bus-type body will stand up to the strains imposed by bad track on these branch lines'.* The unit underwent further trials on a number of other lines including the Chalfont & Latimer branch, the Scottish Region Ayr to Dalmellington branch, the Southern Region Allhallows branch and on the North Eastern Region between Hull and South Howden. It was purchased by British Railways in November 1953 and repainted in lined green when it returned to the St. Albans branch in July 1955.

An ex-L&NWR 'Oerlikon' EMU with No. M28265M leading at Watford Junction on 26th March 1960. The last few of these units spent their final days working the shuttle service from Watford High Street to Croxley Green over the short branch off the ex-LM&SR Watford-Rickmansworth (Church Street) line. In 1951 there were three peak hour services which ran direct from Croxley Green to London avoiding Watford Junction, but only one in the other direction. There were twenty-one shuttle journeys every weekday and the service was taken over by BR-built EMUs in April 1960.

With a Bakerloo Line tube train on the right, Stanier Class '5' No. 45020 blows off steam from its safety valves as it waits to set-off northwards from Watford. It was the very first Class '5' when it emerged from Vulcan Foundry in August 1934. No. 45020 was one of thirteen which received a sloping throatplate boiler in the late-1930s, creating spares of the vertical throatplate type used on the first 225 engines in the class. It has a 2A Rugby shedplate and was allocated there from April 1947 until September 1953 when it was transferred to Edge Hill. The Euston-Watford electrics and the Bakerloo Line trains used four bay platforms to the right of No. 45020 but since 1982 the latter have terminated at Harrow & Wealdstone and all local services to Watford are now provided by the London Overground.

A Permanent Way Look-out man with his flag rolled in a waterproof coat has a cigarette as he stands by the sign warning passengers to cross the line using the bridge as 'Britannia' 4-6-2 No. 70043 *Lord Kitchener* sets off from Watford with a Down express on 25th June 1960. It was one of two of the class built with Westinghouse air brakes, the other being No. 70044. Although allocated to Longsight, they were based at Derby several times during 1953 and 1954 for a number of trials working freight trains on the Midland Main Line, filling in with passenger work down to St. Pancras. The equipment was removed in 1957, and it was named *Lord Kitchener* in 1958. No. 70043 remained at Longsight until early 1962 when it was transferred to Aston.

No. 10001 passing an empty shed with a southbound local between October 1957 and July 1960. It had been repainted in lined green in August 1956 and the aluminium numbers were painted cream and the waist strip eggshell blue in October 1957. In the late 1950s the two LM&SR diesels worked singly on secondary passenger services from Euston to Bletchley, Birmingham/Wolverhampton. No. 10001 continued to work for several years after No. 10000 was stored unserviceable at Derby in November 1962. Components salvaged from its twin were used to keep it operational until March 1966, albeit mainly on local freight work.

No. 10001 approaches the station with a northbound fitted freight on 27th July 1961. Note the two signal boxes which were only a few yards apart. Watford No. 1 is on the left and the one simply named 'Watford' that controlled the electric lines is on the right. Watford No. 2 box was at the north end of the station.

Fairburn 2-6-4T No. 42095 arriving at Watford with an Up stopping train on 13th May 1961. The tank was built at Brighton in June 1951 for the Southern Region and arrived on the London Midland Region from Ashford in December 1959, allocated to Watford. It left for Carlisle Canal in July 1961 and ended its days at Tebay banking trains over Shap.

In the late 1950s and early 1960s Watford Shed always appeared to be almost empty and this was the case on 27th May 1961. There were two Watford engines on their home shed. North British-built '3F' 0-6-0T No. 47355 was there from before nationalisation until withdrawn in October 1964. In the background is '2P' 4-4-0 No. 40672. The part of the building on the left of the picture was built by the L&NWR and that on the right by the LM&SR. Lack of space meant that access to the shed was through a series of headshunts, involving up to five reversals in some instances. The shed was coded '1C' from 1935 until closure in 1965.

Two months later, LM&SR-built '2P'4-4-0 No. 40672 was moving a single bogie bolster for the engineers on 27th July 1961. This engine had been 'Engineer Watford' since 1936 when it took over the role from a former Midland Railway Kirtley 2-4-0 although it did not inherit the latter's nameplates. No. 40672 was withdrawn from Watford in October 1962.

A busy scene viewed from the footbridge, probably during 1962, as English Electric Type '4' No. D288 heads north with a parcels train, passing an Up express on the adjacent line while a BR Sulzer Type '2' waits in the background on the St. Albans line. No. D288 entered service in August 1960 and was withdrawn as No. 40088 in 1982. Watford Junction had twelve platforms, four 'New Line' bays on the western side, Platforms 5 to 9 for the main line, Platforms 10 for the St. Albans branch and 11 to 12 for steam services to and from Euston.

BR Sulzer Type '2' No. D5020 arriving at Watford on an Up Local, taken after it received yellow warning panels in April 1962. The transfer of Nos D5020 and D5021 to Willesden during May 1961 completed the movement of sixteen of the class between the Great Eastern lines and the LMR which enabled the local services out of Euston to be dieselised. No. D5020 was at Willesden until January 1965 when it went to Camden. It moved north, firstly to the Birmingham Division in 1966, then to Stoke in 1967 and finally to Manchester in 1972. It was renumbered as 24020 in April 1974 and was withdrawn in August 1975.

English Electric Type '1' No. D8042 passes Watford Junction with an Up freight in October 1965. It had been transferred to Willesden from Devons Road in February 1964 but would move to Bescot in March 1966. In later days it followed a common pattern for the class, being withdrawn and then subsequently reinstated. When withdrawn for the second time in 1991 it was sold to Pete Waterman's Railway Age in 1993 and subsequently purchased by Direct Rail Services in 1997. After refurbishment at RFS Doncaster, it was renumbered as No. 20312 in 1998 and remains in the DRS fleet today, although not currently operational. *Lewis Coles/Rail Archive Stephenson*

'AL1' No. E3005 passes an empty Watford steam shed as it comes through the station with an Up engineers' train in October 1965. It was withdrawn as No. 81005 in 1989 after suffering severe damage in a collision at Wembley Inter-City depot. *Lewis Coles/Rail Archive Stephenson*

'AL6' electric No. E3112 passes through Watford Junction with a train of new Ford cars (Cortinas, Anglias and Escorts) from the Halewood factory at Liverpool in October 1965. The train is crossing over from the Up Fast to the Up Slow line. No. E3112 was renumbered as No. 86006 in June 1973, No. 86406 in December 1985 and finally to No. 86606 in 1990; it worked until 2001 and was withdrawn in 2003.

Lewis Coles/Rail Archive Stephenson

Watford - St. Albans Abbey

The line was opened in May 1858 by the L&NWR and from its origins as a country branch it increased in importance with new housing development along the route. It survived the 'Beeching axe' and was electrified in 1988 and is now operated by the West Midlands Trains franchise.

In BR lined black livery, push-pull fitted Stanier '2P' 0-4-4T No. 41909 was in front of the St. Albans Branch platform at Watford Junction on 2nd October 1948. Together with No. 41908 it was a regular engine on the branch until replaced in the early 1950s by Fowler and Ivatt 2-6-2Ts. No. 41909 was the last of ten 0-4-4Ts built at Derby in 1932/3 that were credited to William Stanier although ordered before he became CME of the LM&SR in January 1932. They were a slightly updated version of a Midland Railway Johnson design which had last been built in 1900 and it seems certain that they would never have seen the light of day if Stanier had arrived on the LM&SR three months earlier. The engines were originally numbered 6400-6409 but were renumbered in 1946 to make way for new Ivatt Class '2' 2-6-0s. No. 41909 had been allocated to Watford since 1934 and stayed there until September 1955 when it went to Warwick to replace a L&NWR 2-4-2T on the Northampton branch service.

One of the 1955-built ACV three-car railbuses arrives at St. Albans Abbey on 21st April 1957. The prototype set had been trialled on the branch in 1952 and returned for the summer 1955 timetable. The droplight windows of the prototype set were replaced with quarter-lights and the side valances were omitted. *The Railway Observer* commented *'One thing about these railcars which will make them extremely popular is the fascinating unobstructed view of the track ahead obtained from the seat beside the driver'.*

The ACV unit is ready to depart from St. Albans Abbey back to Watford. The 6½ mile journey took fifteen minutes, two minutes less than by steam push-pull. Three extra trains were provided on weekdays, eleven more on Saturdays and eight more on Sundays. The prototype unit was used interchangeably with the new units, but their days were numbered as passenger loadings declined and often a single car would suffice. They suffered reliability problems and by early 1959 were all placed in store at Watford, only to be used 'in cases of extreme emergency'. Conventional diesel multiple units took over until the line was electrified.

4 – St. Pancras

In October 1868 the Midland Railway opened the now-iconic St. Pancras station at the end of the railway's new forty-nine mile London extension south from Bedford. It was built on part of the Somers Estate on the north side of Euston Road and was reached by a raised approach line crossing the Regents Canal which kept the line level into the terminus by using bridges and viaducts. The Victorian neo-Gothic Midland Grand Hotel and station buildings were of red brick and occupied three sides of the train shed. The train shed was designed by William Barlow, the Midland Railway's consulting engineer and had a single 240ft span cast iron. It was 689ft long and 100ft high at the apex and was held up by twenty-five cast iron channel and plate ribs. Below, 720 cast iron columns and girders supported the tracks on Mallet's buckle plates. Underneath, the space at street level was originally rented by the Burton Brewery, hence the distance between the cast iron columns was the same as

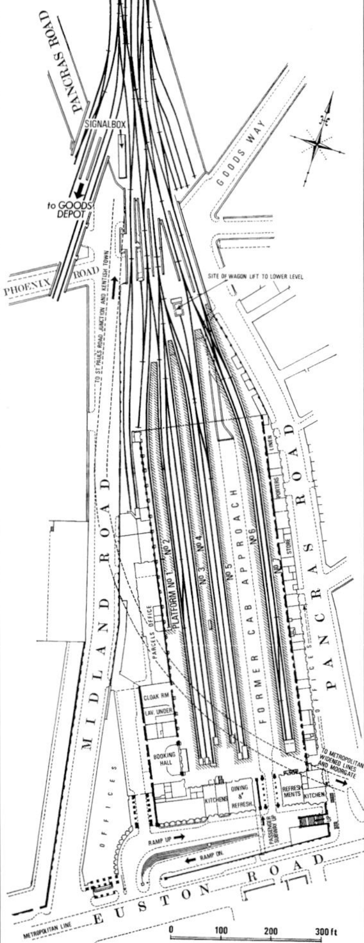

Above: In this picture, looking along Euston Road, the building on the left-hand side with a curved frontage contained the hotel entrance and a large reception area. At the far right is the 270ft high clock tower.

Left: The station layout in 1958 after resignalling and removal of the old signal boxes. Platforms 3 and 4 were the 'infill' platforms added in 1892. The former cab approach was superseded by taxis using the ramps in front of the main façade.

Note the line curving down to the Metropolitan Widened Lines and Moorgate. The Goods Depot referred to on the left is Somers Town – the St. Pancras Goods Depot was a few hundred yards north of the station.

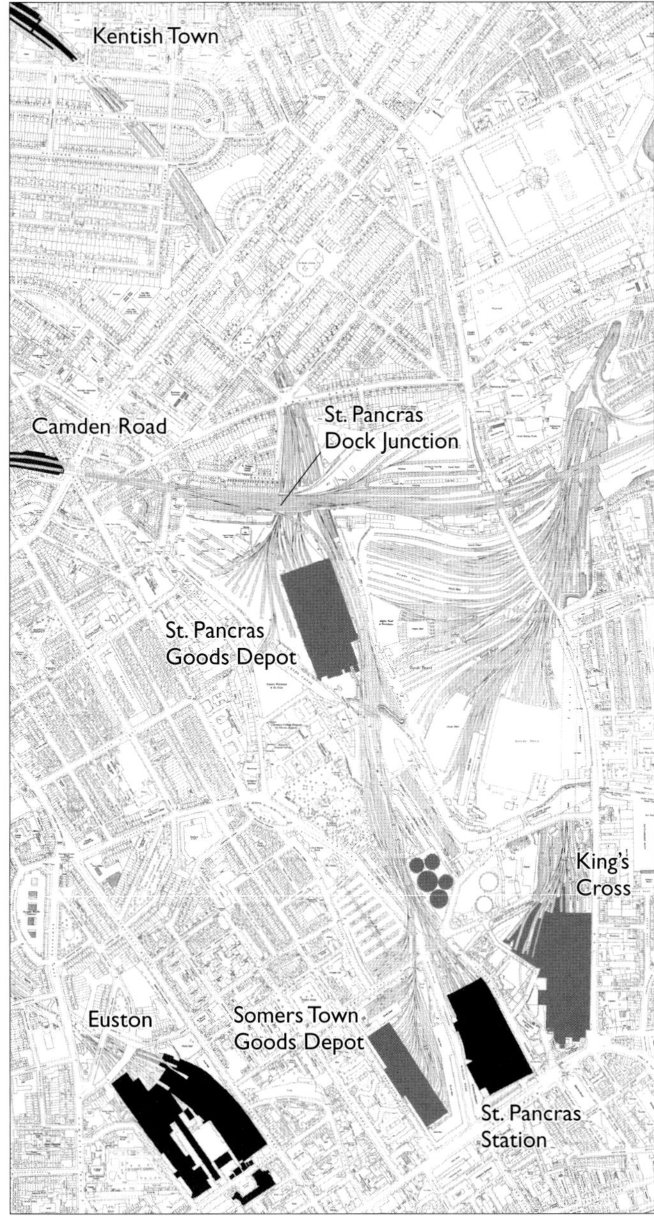

Right: St. Pancras station was situated on the Euston Road, between Euston and King's Cross stations.

in the Burton beer warehouses, so that an exact number of barrels could be fitted in without wasting any space. The hotel and station buildings which were designed by Sir Gilbert Scott comprised three irregular buildings around a great tower with the main façade parallel with Euston Road containing the bedrooms. Behind, in a triangular space separated from the station by an inner road, were offices and the hotel services.

The original station had five platforms and six carriage roads with a 25ft-wide cab road in the centre. In 1892 two additional platforms were added using the carriage roads and from then onwards, little changed over the next century. The approach tracks were rearranged in 1947, British Railways resignalled the station in 1957 and smartened up the passenger areas between 1959 and 1963, but it was not until the end of the 20th century that significant changes were planned when the Channel Tunnel Rail Link Act 1996 authorised the construction of a high-speed link from an enlarged terminal at St. Pancras to the Channel Tunnel. The station had survived two attempts to close it, firstly in the mid-1930s when the LM&SR was planning to rebuild Euston and the plans allowed for capacity to cope with St. Pancras' traffic, and then between 1966 and 1968 there were discussions about combining it with Kings Cross. The latter resulted in the station and hotel being awarded Grade 1 listed building status. Work started in 2004 on extending the train shed to accommodate the Eurostar trains and six additional platforms were added; the meticulously restored station was opened in November 2007. The Hotel, which was closed by the LM&SR in 1935 and had been used as offices for fifty years, was completely refurbished and the undercroft below the platforms was opened up for high-quality retail space.

Steam Days

Midland Railway Johnson '1P' 0-4-4T No. 1382, fitted with a condenser for working in the Metropolitan Widened Line tunnels, stands in one of the centre roads between Platforms 3 and 4 on 10th January 1948. It had been allocated to Cricklewood since Midland Railway days and was renumbered as 58073 in December 1948. It moved to Gloucester Barnwood in March 1953 for two months before ending its days on the Somerset & Dorset at Highbridge.

Two Stanier '3P' 2-6-2Ts from Kentish Town on empty stock work at St. Pancras on 10th June 1948. On the left No. 160, renumbered as No. 40160 in February 1949, was there until withdrawn in November 1959 whereas No. M161 which became No. 40161 in September 1949 moved to Tredegar in South Wales in February 1952. Coaching stock for trains from St. Pancras had to be brought in mainly from Cricklewood Sidings, although there were limited facilities at Kentish Town, and as a result most basic internal servicing was done at the terminus.

'Jubilee' 4-6-0 No. 45565 *Victoria*, in early BR experimental apple green livery with red, cream and grey L&NWR-style lining, departs from St. Pancras with an express for Leeds in 1948. It was one of three of the class from Holbeck repainted at Derby in early 1948 for use on the 9.15am Bradford-St. Pancras and the 4.50pm return which had British Railways' experimental 'plum and split milk' liveried coaching stock. *C.R.L. Coles/Rail Archive Stephenson*

Compound 4-4-0 No. 41095 sets off from St. Pancras on 25th June 1956. Built by the LM&SR in 1925, it was transferred away from Leicester, where it had been since October 1949, to Gloucester Barnwood in May 1957. The tender is a post-war rebuild of a Midland Railway Deeley tender with vertical side sheets. Three of Leicester's Compounds, Nos 41078, 41095 and 41181 regularly worked the 3.20pm St. Pancras-Kettering around this time. Immediately behind the Compound's smokebox is St. Pancras Passenger signal box and to the left is the larger St. Pancras Junction box. The Upper Quadrant signals still have Midland Railway finials.

On Platform 3 the 10.50am express to Leicester is waiting to depart behind BR Standard Caprotti '5MT' 4-6-0 No. 73142 on 13th June 1957. It was at Leicester Midland from new in December 1956, one of five Caprottis there; No. 73142 moved to Derby in January 1959.

On the left is the new power box which came into operation in October 1957, replacing four old boxes including the one on the right, St. Pancras Passenger, which was actually two standard Midland Railway boxes side-by-side and dated from 1900. Its East frame covered Platforms 5, 6 and 7 and the East and West Arrival lines, and the West frame Platforms 1 to 4 and the East and West Departure lines. The signal has been pulled off for 'Jubilee' No. 45667 *Jellicoe* to depart on 12th July 1957. It had been a Midland Division engine since 1937 and was at Nottingham from September 1952 until November 1961, apart from two brief loan spells at Trafford Park.

'2P' 4-4-0 No. 40580 on ECS duty according to the lamps on 13th April 1958. It was one of the later LM&SR-built engines, entering service in October 1929. No. 40590 had been in North Wales from 1951 until December 1957 when it was transferred to Kentish Town, where it stayed until withdrawal in February 1961.

Stanier '3P' 2-6-2T No. 40203 probably with empty coaching stock on 28th October 1960. Built in February 1938, it was fitted with a larger boiler in 1942, one of six of the class modified in an attempt to improve their poor performance. However, even after this the engines remained the weakest of the Stanier standard types, probably because they were still heavy in relation to their tractive effort. No. 40203 had arrived at Kentish Town in September 1959 from Brunswick shed in Liverpool and was withdrawn from there in July 1962. It replaced another large boilered engine, No. 40167 which had moved from Kentish Town to Leicester in January of that year.

'Royal Scot' 4-6-0 No. 46118 *Royal Welch Fusilier* about to depart with 'The Waverley' from St. Pancras on 9th July 1960. It had arrived on the Midland Division at the end of 1959 as part of the transfer of displaced rebuilt '7P' 4-6-0s from the Western Division to the Midland Division in 1959/60. No. 46118 moved from Camden to Kentish Town along with seven other Royal Scots and a rebuilt 'Patriot' in late 1959. 'The Waverley' left London at 9.15am and arrived in Edinburgh Waverley 9¼ hours later after a scenic journey over both the Settle & Carlisle and Waverley lines. This was the last summer in which it was steam worked, diesels taking over at the start of the 1961 summer timetable.

Although carrying Class 'D' freight lamps, Fowler 2-6-4T No. 42335 is more likely about to take out empty coaching stock on 6th August 1960. It was at Kentish Town for just over two years, from January 1960 until August 1962.

The mail has not yet been loaded as 'Jubilee' No. 45614 *Leeward Islands* waits for departure on 18th March 1961. It spent most of its working life at Kentish Town, punctuated by short loan spells to the Manchester sheds at Newton Heath and Trafford Park, eventually leaving for Derby in December 1961.

Boat trains to Tilbury (Riverside) ran from St. Pancras for many years, from 1894 up to April 1963 when they were replaced by EMUs working from Fenchurch Street. The trains for shipping lines such as P&O, Orient Line and Swedish Lloyd ran via the Tottenham & Forest Gate Joint line to join the LT&S at Woodgrange Park near Barking. Ivatt Class '4' 2-6-0 No. 43121 was working a Swedish Lloyd special on 11th July 1961, a regular duty for the engines of this class based at Cricklewood in the 1950s. The four engines including No. 43121 were mostly used on transfer freight work but turned their hand to passenger duties when required. No. 43121 went to Cricklewood from new in August 1951 and was there until September 1962. Swedish Lloyd insisted on specially cleaned and marshalled stock.

The driver of Fowler '3P' 2-6-2T No. 40031 has just finished oiling his engine on 21st August 1961. It was built in March 1931 with condensing apparatus for working in the Metropolitan Widened Line tunnels and was at Kentish Town from September 1949 until withdrawn in November 1962, except for a few months at Cricklewood in mid-1960.

The new power signalling box at the end of Platform 1 was opened in October 1957 following the installation of two- and four-aspect colour light signalling and electro-pneumatic points. It controlled the tracks out to the far side of Belsize Tunnel and, unusually, its full-height windows had draw blinds to protect the view into the sun. The stub track to the right of the train led to the hydraulic wagon hoist down to the beer vaults beneath the station that was in use until 1960. Note the wooden stop block and flange detector on the approach road to show the signalman if a wagon had been left foul. On 22nd August 1961 'Jubilee' No. 45620 *North Borneo* is arriving from Nottingham where it had been allocated since December 1949. It was one of fifty of the class built with the smaller 3,500 gallon version of the standard Stanier tender and it kept the same tender until withdrawn in September 1964.

Two 'Jubilee's double-head an express from Sheffield in May 1962. Leading is No. 45656 *Cochrane* which had been allocated to Millhouses from November 1951 until the end of 1961 when it moved to nearby Canklow. The engines are crossing the bridge over the Old Pancras Road and behind them tower the gasholders of the former Imperial Gas, Light and Coke Company which had been operating from the site since 1824, and at one time the largest gasworks in the world. They were decommissioned in 2000 and, after dismantling, one of the four 100ft diameter 85ft high Grade II Listed structures was rebuilt and positioned slightly further north alongside the canal as the centrepiece in what is now 'Gasholder Park'. Next to this, the other three were also rebuilt and now house luxury apartments that were built inside the structures, in a development entitled 'Gasholders London'.

Diesels

Metropolitan-Vickers Co-Bo No. D5713 with a classmate at St. Pancras on 3rd September 1959. When first introduced they were used in pairs on trains between St. Pancras and Manchester but within a short time they began to suffer frequent breakdowns. By early 1960, the Class was suffering frequent mechanical failures, and just three of the twenty were available for traffic, with the others stored at Derby and Cricklewood. Many were declared unserviceable whilst British Railways and the manufacturers argued over who should pay to make the locomotives more reliable. After the two parties eventually agreed on the necessary course of action, they began to be returned to Metropolitan-Vickers' works at Dukinfield, Manchester to receive modifications to the troublesome Crossley diesel engines and a general overhaul. Nos D5707 and D5713 were the first in mid-1961 and the rest followed two at a time. All were transferred to Barrow in February 1962 and did not return to the Midland Main Line when they left Dukinfield. The modifications were to no avail because the Class was deemed non-standard under the 1967 British Railways Traction Plan.

The wrap-around cab windows show up clearly in this view of No. D5713 waiting to depart from St. Pancras in 1959. Whilst undergoing their modification work back at their Dukinfield builders these windows were replaced with new window frames welded inside the originals and a more robust rubber seal installed to hold the now flat window glass in place. Although they looked quite stylish and offered good forward views for the train crew, they had been susceptible to dropping out at high speed due to excessive vibration. No. D5713 went into service in March 1959 and was withdrawn at the end of 1967, having spent over a year in works during that time. At a cost of £78,437 each, the 'Metro-Vicks' probably represented the worst value for the taxpayers' money of any of the diesel types ordered under the Modernisation Plan.

A brand new Derby four-car suburban unit, with Driving Motor Brake Second No. M51604 leading, waits to leave St. Pancras with the 4.25pm to Derby on what was probably a 'running-in' turn on 8th August 1959. These units were fitted with Rolls-Royce engines and had hydraulic rather than the mechanical transmission which was used in the other first generation DMUs. The full diesel service between St. Pancras and Bedford was introduced in January 1960 following much preparatory work including upgrading of the goods lines between Harpenden and Bedford, lengthening of platforms at some stations to accommodate eight-car trains, improvements to station amenities, signalling and permanent way and the construction of a new maintenance depot at Cricklewood. The new timetable had one train leaving St. Pancras on the hour every hour for all stations to Luton, and one at thirty-five minutes past for Elstree and all stations onwards to Bedford. In the opposite direction, the semi-fasts from Bedford and the stopping trains from Luton all left on the hour, resulting in a half-hourly service to and from Leagrave, Harlington and Flitwick. Unfortunately, as happened with other new BR traction, there were numerous teething difficulties with trains cancelled or curtailed. Although the allocation of thirty sets included four spares these proved insufficient, and additional DMUs were brought in and steam even had to substitute on some services. *Lewis Coles/Rail Archive Stephenson*

The ten pilot scheme BR Sulzer Type '4's were used intermittently on St. Pancras-Manchester trains from late 1959 until early 1961 when they were superseded by the squadron introduction of the more powerful production series. No. D7 *Ingleborough* backs out after the train it had brought in has departed. It was initially at Camden working on the West Coast Main Line but was loaned to the Midland Division at the end of 1959 for four months; it returned permanently in February 1962 when the 'Ten' were all banished to Toton for freight work. By this time their more powerful successors had taken over the Midland Division passenger work. At the end of February 1961 the diesel-hauled passenger workings out of St. Pancras included the services to Derby, Manchester, Nottingham and Leeds, made possible by the growing number of 'Peak's delivered from Derby and Crewe; full dieselisation had been officially scheduled for April 1961. However, in the first few months there were frequent failures and the 'Royal Scots' and 'Jubilee's which had been relegated to the semi-fasts returned to the expresses until the diesels had settled down and more were delivered.

No. D128 runs into St. Pancras, probably in 1967 or 1968 since the train has a number of blue and grey liveried coaches. In the 1968 Working Timetable train '1C55' was the 14.00 Nottingham-St. Pancras, due in at 16.11, the coaches forming the 1E15 17.05 working to Sheffield. The 'Peak' has a central headcode box split into two – introduced with No. D31 from Crewe and No. D108 from Derby. No. D128 became No. 45145 in December 1974 when fitted with electric train heating. It worked on the Midland Lines until November 1986 when it moved to Tinsley for its last year in service.

Although full servicing for the diesels was carried out at Cricklewood, basic refuelling facilities were constructed at Cambridge Street, adjacent to St. Pancras, opening in January 1961, where No. D79 was photographed. The condition of its paintwork suggests that this was soon after it was one of around twenty of the class repainted at Toton in summer 1966 in blue with small yellow warning panels but old-style serif numbers and no BR emblems. It was classified as a '45/0' under TOPS because it was not fitted with electric train heating equipment and became No. 45005 late 1973.

'Peak' Type '4' No. D38 after arrival in Platform 5 on 9th June 1968. The Post Office van and the parcels trolleys are on the former cab approach which gave the interior a much more spacious feel than in other London termini. The digital clock shows 13.27 but the magnificent clock on the windscreen has lost its hands, although they would be replaced when the clock was restored to its former glory half a century later in the International station.

BR Sulzer Type '4' No. D54 *The Royal Pioneer Corps* with the 13.05 St. Pancras-Sheffield on 9th June 1968. It was built at Derby in August 1962 and named at St. Pancras in November 1963. It became No. 45023 in January 1975 and worked until September 1984. Note the 'M' for Midland Lines below the stock number.

Class '127' Motor Brake Second No. M51643 on a Luton service in the early 1970s. The 1959 Derby-built units soldiered on until April 1983 when the 'Bed-Pan' electrification was completed, delayed by almost a year because of a dispute with the ASLEF trade union over driver-only operation. In fact, some of the units continued to work peak-hour services for several months after this.

The Midland Pullman

The 'Midland Pullman' at St. Pancras in 1960. It is 12.39pm and the train is ready to leave at 12.45pm on its filling-in run to Leicester and back (in January 1961 the service was extended to Nottingham). Designed and built by Metropolitan-Cammell of Birmingham, these luxury Pullman trains were introduced on the Midland Division in July 1960 while the West Coast Main Line was being electrified. Two six-car First Class-only sets were built but only one was used each day for the 3¼ hours journey between Manchester Central and St. Pancras, the other being kept as 'spare'. The striking livery of Nanking Blue was relieved by a broad band of white extending the length of the windowed section along the side of each car. The Pullman Company crest was carried on the nose-end of the power cars. The reign of the 'Midland Pullman' was short-lived because once the Euston-Manchester electrification was completed the sets were transferred to the Western Region in April 1966 and replaced by locomotive-hauled Pullmans running to Manchester Piccadilly and Liverpool.

On the same day as the picture above the 'Midland Pullman' pulls out of St. Pancras for its run to Leicester. The in-fill working was nicknamed 'the empty stock' by railwaymen because of its poor patronage.

5 – Midland Division Sheds

Kentish Town

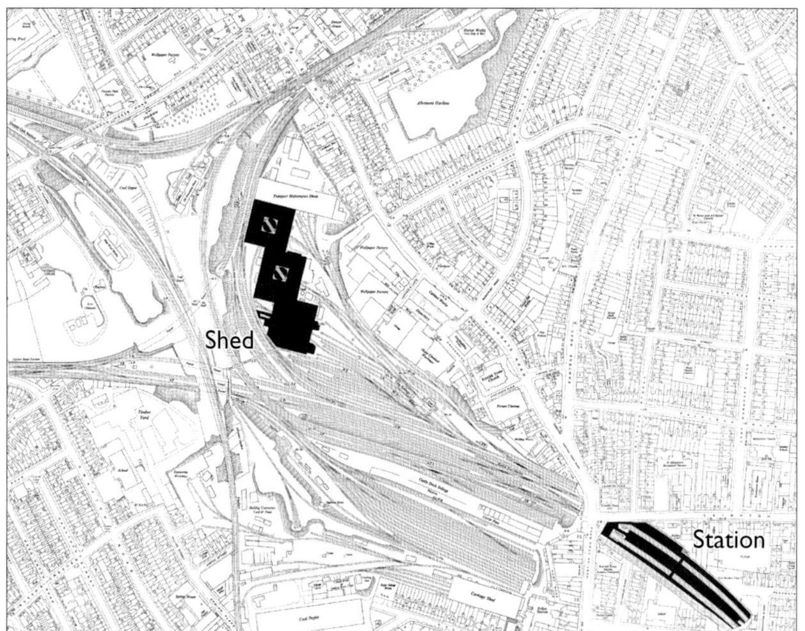

Kentish Town was opened in 1868 when the Midland Railway London extension was completed. It had two roundhouses and a further two were added in 1899 when one of the original sheds had to be demolished to accommodate the widening of the adjacent main line. Until the 1930s it had a comprehensive fitting or erecting shop and a paint shop, reflecting the shed's status as the principal London depot of the Midland Railway. It had an allocation of all the prevailing express classes and serviced visiting passenger locomotives. There were also tank engines for the local services out of St. Pancras and for traffic through the tunnels to Moorgate, for which the engines involved were fitted with condensing apparatus. The coal and ash handling equipment were modernised in 1939/40. In 1954 Kentish Town had ninety-nine engines on its books, ranging from 'Jubilees' to three MR '1F' 0-6-0Ts which contrasted with four brand-new BR Standard 2-6-4Ts. Dieselisation of the Midland Main Line had an early impact with the final few steam survivors in store by November 1962. The shed was coded 14B by the LM&SR and British Railways and was closed in April 1963.

Condenser-fitted Fowler '3P' 2-6-2T No. 40036 had received its BR number in July 1948, two months before this picture was taken, using large LM&SR block style cab numbers and smokebox number plate. It was allocated to Kentish Town until April 1960 when it was transferred, on paper at least, to Cricklewood and was swiftly withdrawn at the end of May. No. 40036 is standing in front of the Read Brothers Limited Bottling Store – in 1906 they were the largest buyers and bottlers of Bass Ale in the world, all sold for export. On the roof line of the rectangular flat-roofed brick building on the right was 'Dog's Head Brand – Bottled Beers', bottled for Australia. A siding ran into the works from the railway.

1950s

A nice detail shot of what were known by enthusiasts as 'half-cabs', Johnson '1F' 0-6-0T No. 41713 in the open roofed No. 1 roundhouse on 15th June 1955. This shed was used for tank locomotives and was known as the 'Metro'. No. 41713 has a hand painted front number below where the cast number plate would be positioned. It was one of the class not to be rebuilt with a Belpaire boiler which probably contributed to its withdrawal two months after this picture was taken. No. 41713 was a Kentish Town engine from before nationalisation.

Kentish Town shed was hemmed in on all sides and behind 'Jubilee' No. 45658 *Keyes* on 15th June 1955 is the Church of St. John and the Forum Cinema. *Keyes* was the only 'Jubilee' to remain at one shed during its whole working life; it was at Holbeck from December 1934 until September 1965 and had the highest recorded mileage of the class at 1,728,870 miles. The Church of St. John in the background became redundant in 1993 and was then used for all-night raves but since 2011 it has been the Nigerian Pentecostal religion's Christ Apostolic Church.

1960s

The preserved Midland 'Compound' No. 1000 at Kentish Town on 24th April 1960 had worked an Ian Allan excursion to Doncaster Works with the Great Western Railway *City of Truro* on 20th April; on the return journey the GWR engine failed with a hot axlebox and No. 1000 completed the journey alone. Built in 1902 it was the first Midland Railway engine to use the Smith system of compounding. When it was withdrawn in September 1951 it was left in the open at Derby, and eventually in August 1953 was moved to Crewe Works for storage in the Paint Shop. No. 1000 remained there until March 1959 when it went to Derby for restoration to working order. This was completed in August 1959 putting the Compound back to its 1914 Deeley condition when the engine was rebuilt with a superheated G9AS boiler. It was used on special trains and excursions until 1963, and then spent twelve years in Clapham Museum before transfer to the National Railway Museum in 1975 where it was overhauled. No. 1000 ran on the main lines of British Rail until 1983 before being retired again in the National Railway Museum.

With the coaling tower on the right, Holbeck 'Jubilee' No. 45566 *Queensland* on 14th June 1962. It was at the Leeds shed from 1940 until withdrawal in November 1962. The signs for Read Brothers Limited Bottling Store and the painted 'Dog's Head Brand – Bottled Beers' are still there, although the latter is somewhat faded.

'Royal Scot' No. 46143 *The South Staffordshire Regiment* was one of the former Western Division engines transferred to the Midland in 1959/60. It went to Trafford Park in December 1960 and was there until September 1962 when it moved to Annesley to see out its final year on the former Great Central line. In the background is Kentish Town church on the left and on the right the rear of the Art Deco Forum Cinema which was built in 1934 and given Grade II listed status in 1990. After closure in the 1970s it was used firstly as a dance hall and a bingo hall before becoming a live music venue in the 1980s. It was renovated in 2007 and is now the 'O2 Forum Kentish Town'.

Birmingham Railway Carriage & Wagon Company Type '2' No. D5381 alongside a classmate on 5th June 1962. It entered service on 1st May allocated to Cricklewood. Thirty-seven of these locomotives were delivered there between March and September 1962. By the first week of April the first three, Nos D5379/80/81, had arrived. Their duties were varied, for example in May pairs of them were diagrammed for a morning Nottingham - St. Pancras passenger, returning at noon to Nottingham. They were noted on empty coaching stock workings around St. Pancras, parcels workings and Moorgate services, and took over London area freight work including the cross-London transfer freights. Their stay in the Capital was less than a decade and by 1970 all had been transferred to Scotland, some via the East Midlands and some directly. No. D5381 was one of the former, going to the Nottingham Division in June 1968 and then to Eastfield in May 1973; it was withdrawn as No. 27033 in 1986.

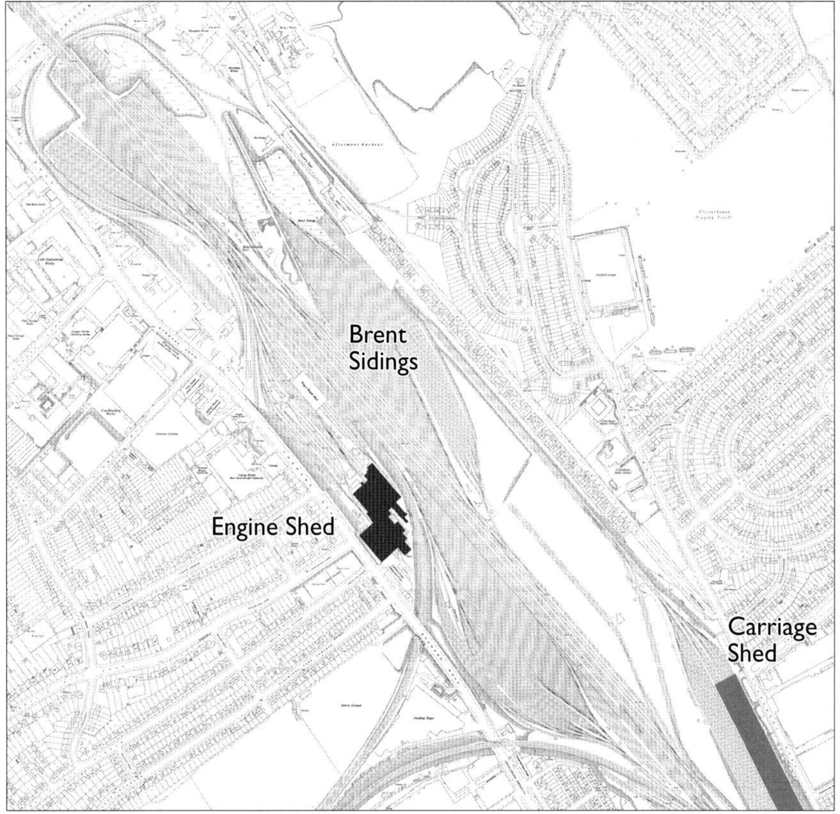

Cricklewood

Cricklewood shed was 5½ miles from St. Pancras opposite Brent Sidings and it supplied the shunting engines for the yard as well as the engines fitted with condensing apparatus for working through the Metropolitan Widened Line tunnels. The shed had two roundhouses, the first built in 1882 and the second in 1893 as the traffic to the nearby Brent Sidings continued to increase. Its allocation for many years consisted of Midland Railway 0-6-0s and 0-6-0Ts with a small number of 0-4-4 passenger tanks. From the late 1920s larger locomotives appeared, 0-8-0s and 'Garratts' from the northern sheds visited on freight work and Fowler 2-6-2Ts took over passenger duties. After the Second World War, Stanier '8F' 2-8-0s arrived on the allocation followed by BR '9F' 2-10-0s in the mid-1950s. The LM&SR installed new mechanical coal and ash handling equipment in the 1930s and both roundhouses were given new concrete roofs by British Railways. A new diesel maintenance depot opened on the east side of the main line in 1959 and in September 1963 it took over the steam shed's 14A code, the latter becoming 14B Cricklewood West. Steam was banished from December 1964 and the old shed continued as a diesel stabling point until 1969 when it was demolished and the site cleared.

Steam

The depot had a number of the Midland Railway '3F' 0-6-0Ts with condensing apparatus for working through the Metropolitan Widened Line tunnels. No. 47209 at Cricklewood on 1st May 1954 would move on to Kentish Town at the end of 1955. It was built for the Midland Railway by Vulcan Foundry in 1900 and was withdrawn in April 1961.

Midland Railway built '4F' 0-6-0 No. 43947 alongside the ash plant at its home shed on 20th June 1954. It was fitted with Hudd ATC equipment to allow it to work over the London Tilbury & Southend lines; the protection plate and reservoir show up clearly here as the fireman cleans out the firebox from the pit.

Midland Railway Johnson '1F' 0-6-0T No. 41712 inside the shed on 20th June 1954 with '3F' condensing tank No. 47251 behind. At nationalisation, both engines were on Cricklewood's books; the '1F' stayed until the end of 1956 when it moved to Nottingham while No. 47251 was there until withdrawn in August 1958.

Above: Beyer-Garratt 2-6-6-2T No. 47970 at rest next to '4F' No. 44297 on 11th April 1955 was built by Beyer, Peacock as LM&SR No. 4970 in August 1930, and renumbered as No. 7970 in August 1939. It was taken out of service a month after this picture was taken after reaching 559,577 miles in service, around the average for the class. No 'Garratts' were allocated to Cricklewood although they did have to be serviced there each day before they returned north.

'Jubilee' No. 45620 *North Borneo* and '9F' 2-10-0 No. 92119 in steam on 28th April 1962. No. 92119 was from Leicester Midland, where it was allocated from April 1959 until March 1965. No. 45620 had been transferred to Burton from Nottingham in November 1961.

Diesels

A new maintenance depot was opened at the end of 1959 primarily to service the new DMUs introduced in January 1960 on the suburban services out of St. Pancras. It was sited on the opposite side of the main line to the steam shed and adjacent to the carriage sidings. One of the depot's four-car units was there on 12th January 1960. It appears to have employed a rather unusual building technique, delivering a first phase operational shed before continuing with the construction of another three bays on the right.

'Metro-Vick' Type '2' No. D5714 parked with classmate No. D5715 at the steam shed, possibly when all except three of the class of twenty were stored in early 1960 following frequent mechanical failures. Many were declared unserviceable whilst BR and the manufacturers argued over who should pay to make the locomotives more reliable. No. D5714 went to Dukinfield for modification in October 1961 and was there until November 1962; it spent a further year in Crewe Works from October 1965 until October 1966 and was finally put out of its misery in September 1968. Note the incorrectly facing BR crest and the stencilled 17A Derby shed code on the buffer beam.

An altogether more successful design was the Type '2' built by the Birmingham Railway Carriage & Wagon Company. Fresh from the factory at Smethwick No. D5386 was inside the depot in May 1962. It entered service on 18th May allocated to Cricklewood and was there until October 1963, transferring to Leicester, before returning to Cricklewood in June 1964. No. D5386 went back to Leicester in January 1965 and then moved to Scotland at Eastfield in October 1969. It was renumbered as No. 27103 in April 1974 when it was modified for the Glasgow-Edinburgh push-pull service, No. 27212 in March 1975 and finally to No. 27066 in November 1982. It was in service until July 1987 and was then purchased for preservation by the North Norfolk Railway who sold it to the Keith & Dufftown Railway in 2002. It is now at Barrow Hill.

Brand new BR Sulzer Type '2' diesels Nos D5194 and D5193 with a less than pristine brake tender had been officially in traffic for only a few days when photographed on 11th May 1963. Under TOPS, they became Nos 25044 and 25043 respectively and were in service until the 1980s.

Gloucester Railway Carriage & Wagon Co. single unit parcels van No. M55989 refuels at what was then called Cricklewood East on 1st May 1966. It was one of four non-gangwayed parcels units built for the London Midland Region and was powered by two Leyland Albion 6-cylinder engines developing 238 bhp. They had three pairs of sliding doors on each side on a 64ft 6in. underframe and both ends were split into two with a half-cab for the driver and half for the guard's area leaving 55ft for parcels use. The units had a four-character headcode panel beneath the centre front window and were originally allocated to Newton Heath but moved away almost immediately. In the background is a small part of Brent Sidings.

6 – St. Pancras to St. Albans

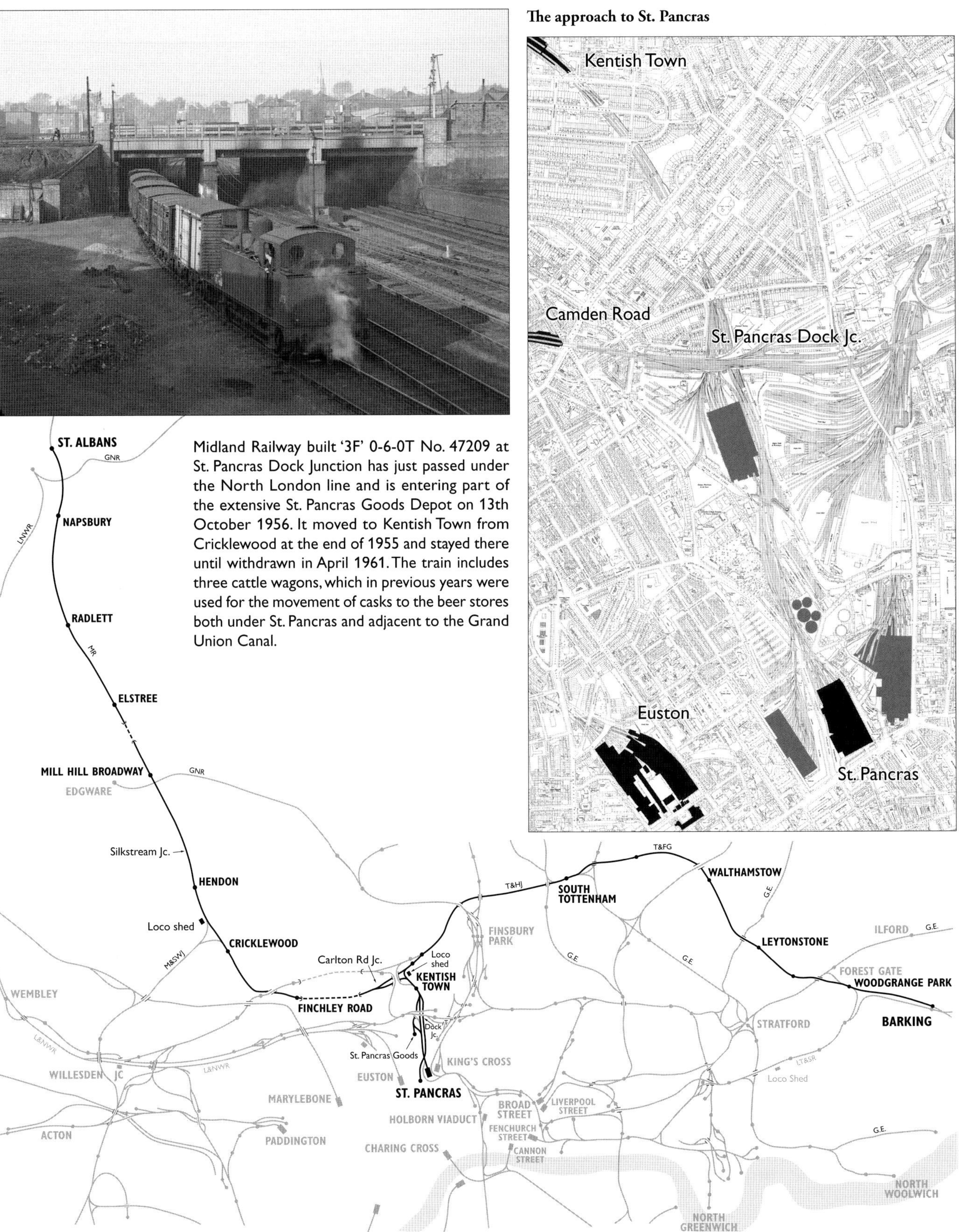

Midland Railway built '3F' 0-6-0T No. 47209 at St. Pancras Dock Junction has just passed under the North London line and is entering part of the extensive St. Pancras Goods Depot on 13th October 1956. It moved to Kentish Town from Cricklewood at the end of 1955 and stayed there until withdrawn in April 1961. The train includes three cattle wagons, which in previous years were used for the movement of casks to the beer stores both under St. Pancras and adjacent to the Grand Union Canal.

Kentish Town

Large boilered Stanier Class '3' 2-6-2T No. 40203 on an Up stopping passenger at Kentish Town on 14th October 1959. No. 40203 had arrived at Kentish Town in September 1959 from Brunswick Shed in Liverpool and had replaced another large boilered engine, No. 40167, which had moved from Kentish Town to Leicester in January 1959.

Just arrived from Barking via the Tottenham & Forest Gate Joint line and about to set back onto the Down line is Fowler 2-6-2T No. 40053 on 30th December 1959. It had been transferred to Kentish Town from Willesden three weeks before this picture was taken.

A few days later than the picture overleaf and working the same service, No. 40053 on 6th January 1960 has just set back onto the Barking platform and will now run round the train. No. 40053 was at Kentish Town for less than a year, leaving for Bedford in November 1960 and was withdrawn there in July 1961. DMUs took over the Kentish Town-Barking service on 11th January, running to an hourly regular interval timetable.

On the same day as the picture above, Stanier '3P' 2-6-2T No. 40142 with an Up stopping passenger train. It had been fitted with a large boiler, during 1956, joining No. 40167 which had been similarly treated, at Kentish Town.

Fairburn 2-6-4T No. 42134 sets off from Kentish Town on 8th January 1960 with a Down stopping passenger service. It was allocated to St. Albans from new in January 1950 and was transferred to Cricklewood during the week ending 16th January 1960, but its stay there was brief and it moved to Neasden four months later.

A former Western Region high-density Derby three-car Class '116' DMU at Kentish Town in the 1970s. A number of these sets were transferred to Cricklewood in 1968/9 and the early 1970s to replace the Rolls-Royce-engined Class '127' units on the City Widened Lines services following the removal of vehicle length restrictions.

Kentish Town to Barking

The Midland Main Line was linked to the LT&S via a route from Kentish Town to Woodgrange Park west of Barking. The line ran through South Tottenham (where it connected with the Great Eastern Railway), Walthamstow and Leytonstone, and was built in two halves. The first, opened in 1868, was built by the Tottenham & Hampstead Junction Railway which was owned jointly by the Midland and Great Eastern Railways. After a slow start, traffic built up and in 1894 it was connected to the newly completed Tottenham & Forest Gate Railway which was also jointly owned, this time between the Midland and the LT&SR. In the 1923 Grouping the T&FG came wholly under the LM&SR while the T&HJR was under the joint ownership of the LM&SR and the L&NER. The overall route was used not only for freight between the Midland lines, the GER lines and the LT&S and the Kentish Town-Barking passenger service, but also by the boat trains from St. Pancras to Tilbury as well as excursion traffic to and from the LT&S. Although there were a number of different MR and GER local services in the late 19th and early 20th century, by the mid-1920s the only remaining service was between Kentish Town and Barking. Today, the passenger service on the line is part of the London Overground network running between Gospel Oak and Barking.

Hughes-Fowler 2-6-0 No. 42794 at South Tottenham in the early 1950s is signalled to go off down the Tottenham & Forest Gate line to Barking and the LT&S. It was built in 1927 as LM&SR No. 13094, renumbered as 2794 in 1934 and was given its BR number in October 1948 during a 'Heavy General' repair. No. 42794 was at Cricklewood from December 1947 until November 1954 when it was transferred to Sheffield Grimesthorpe. The station was originally 'South Tottenham & Stamford Hill' becoming plain 'South Tottenham' in 1949.

Midland Railway Johnson '2F' 0-6-0 No. 58158 has not taken the fork to the left onto the T&FG line at Tottenham, but will turn at the West Junction to join the former GER tracks at the South Junction and go south towards Stratford via Copper Mill Junction. No. 58158 was at Kentish Town from May 1948 until March 1954 when it moved to Derby. There is some nice detail of the point rodding and note that the ex-private owner wagon still has grease axleboxes.

A BRC&W Type '2' diesel-electric has left the Midland Main Line at Kentish Town, travelled through Harringay Park Station and passes under the former Great Eastern Railway line from Hackney Downs and Bethnal Green with an eastbound freight from Brent Sidings on 27th September 1962. The train is approaching South Tottenham Station and the sharp curve which branches off joins the Great Eastern line to the right of the EMU which has just left Seven Sisters Station and is heading for the overbridge and then on to Liverpool Street. The curve was closed to passengers in January 1963 when the North Woolwich-Palace Gates service which used it was withdrawn and it was singled in 1977, although later re-opened to passenger services.

Finchley Road

A view eastward on 28th February 1953 from the path beside the North London Line between Finchley Road & Frognal and West End Lane stations, where the NLR crosses the Midland Main Line out of St. Pancras. All the lines are emerging from tunnels (Hampstead Tunnel on the North London off to the left, Belsize Tunnel on the Midland ahead; also off to the right are the tunnels of the LT Metropolitan lines from Baker Street at Finchley Road (LT) and beyond it the ex-Great Central line from Marylebone. On the Down Fast line, Kentish Town 'Jubilee' No. 45648 *Wemyss* on a stopping train from St. Pancras to Bedford is passing the remains of Finchley Road Midland station (closed in 1927). On the left an empty stock train heading for St. Pancras is about to join the Up Fast line into the tunnel. On the right are the Goods lines, using their own tunnel then the goods yards of the Midland and Metropolitan (also a Cadbury's warehouse); out of picture on the right are the four London Transport tracks and finally the two L&NER (ex-Great Central) tracks. It must have been a great spot for the enthusiast.

Fairburn 2-6-4T No. 42685 running Light Engine at Finchley Road was a Midland Division engine from new in April 1946 until withdrawn in September 1962. It was at Kentish Town from November 1954 until July 1962 when it moved to Rowsley. This picture was taken looking east from a passing train on the North London Line viaduct between Finchley Road & Frognall and West Hampstead stations. In the distance, directly above the engine's bunker, is Finchley Road London Transport station. The large building in the far centre background is St. Johns Court flats which date from 1938.

The 'Midland Pullman', probably the mid-day 'filler' service from Leicester to St. Pancras on the Up Fast at Finchley Road in 1961. The low building by the sidings is the Cadbury's depot. There were usually a number of fitted vans there emblazoned with the legend 'Return Empty to Bournville'. There is a wonderful collection of period vehicles on the right and clutter in the brick-built transfer bins on the left. The truck is an Austin K8.

On 27th February 1952 BR Standard Class '5' 4-6-0 No. 73019 leans into the curve on the Down Fast between Finchley Road and West Hampstead and is about to pass underneath the North London Line whose Finchley Road signal box is visible in the left background. No. 73019 was on home territory, allocated to Nottingham from new in October 1951 until transferred to Bristol in October 1953. In the distance on the right is the Goods Lines portal of Belsize Tunnel and on the left the coaches are probably stabled in a couple of sidings used for that purpose.

Cricklewood

Still with its cast aluminium LMS lettering diesel-electric No. 10000 heads the 2.15pm from St. Pancras at Watling Street Junction south of Cricklewood on 24th April 1948. It was rostered for a few months on a Derby-St. Pancras diagram covering two return trips each day on which it clocked up a weekly mileage of 3,084. *Ben Brooksbank*

Ivatt 2-6-2T No. 1207 still in LMS livery at Cricklewood working a St. Pancras - St. Albans service on 18th June 1948. It was observed on Kentish Town-Barking trains and empty stock workings out of St. Pancras soon after it entered service at the end of 1946, allocated to Kentish Town. No. 1207 was transferred to Cricklewood in November 1949 and remained there until June 1956 when it left London for the West Country at Bristol Barrow Road.

A Football Special from Leicester for the 1961 FA Cup Final, which Leicester City lost to Tottenham Hotspur, passing through Cricklewood Station on the Up Fast behind 'Jubilee' No. 45650 *Blake* on 6th May 1961. No. 45650 was at Leicester between January 1960 and June 1961 when it was loaned to Newton Heath for a few weeks; it left permanently for Burton in November. There were sixteen specials from Leicester to the Cup Final that day, seven of which were worked by 'Jubilees'.

Sheffield Millhouses rebuilt 'Patriot' No. 45536 *Private W. Wood, V.C.* with an Up express on 6th May 1961. It was built in 1933 as LM&SR No. 6018 and was given the name of the L&NWR 'Claughton' it replaced, one of two 'Patriots' to carry the name of an L&NWR employee who had received the Victoria Cross. It became LM&SR No. 5536 in April 1934 and was rebuilt with a tapered boiler in November 1948. On the extreme right is part of the Express Dairy plant that processed milk for the Capital from as far afield as Scotland and Cumberland. To the left of the bracket signal are the lines branching off forming the start of the MR route to Acton Wells Junction, the route to south London. Beyond these is the start of Brent Yard, the primary destination for the numerous mineral trains from the Midlands coalfields. Even in 1961 Midland Railway infrastructure predominates, from the signal box to the lamp posts. There are some Midland Railway signals beyond the train although the main bracket is an early LM&SR product based on L&NWR practice but topped by LM&SR upper-quadrant arms.

Two photographers capture Class '45' No. 132 passing through with a Down parcels train on 3rd January 1973. It became No. 45075 under TOPS and was in service until January 1985. Cricklewood goods depot was closed in October 1969 but the station is still open today and enjoys a frequent Thameslink service.

Hendon

LM&SR diesel-electric No. 10000 approaching Hendon on the 8.55am from Derby on 23rd February 1948. This was its first day of regular revenue earning service. It returned to Derby with the 2.15pm from St. Pancras.

'Metro-Vick' Co-Bos Nos D5701 and D5704 adorned with the 'Condor' cast headboard back down onto the 'Condor' container train that is standing in Hendon station ready for the ten-hour overnight run to Glasgow on 7th July 1959. The service between Hendon and Gushetfaulds started on 16th March. It cost £16 for a small container and £18 for a large size. The full load was twenty-seven roller-bearing container flat wagons, weighing 550 tons. After a few months, the load was reduced to thirteen wagons powered by a single locomotive. *K.L. Cook/Rail Archive Stephenson*

'Metro-Vick' Co-Bos Nos D5701 and D5704 set off from Hendon with the 'Condor' on 7th July 1959 in a cloud of diesel fumes from their Crossley 8-cylinder engines. The train ran to Glasgow (Gushetfaulds) via Leeds, Settle and Carlisle. Departure in the Up direction from Glasgow was at 7.35pm Sundays and 7.50pm (FSX) The Down service left Hendon at 7.23pm. Arrival times were 5.15am at Gushetfaulds and 5.40am at Hendon. The reliability of the Co-Bos was such that instructions were soon produced stating that in the event of one locomotive failure, a Class '5' 4-6-0 should deputise with the diesel piloting; if both locomotives failed two 4-6-0s were to be used. *K. L. Cook/Rail Archive Stephenson*

Silkstream Junction

A St. Pancras to Luton semi-fast on 25th May 1957 headed by Stanier 2-6-4T No. 42595 at Silkstream Junction, passing under the flyover, known as the 'Hendon Crossing', which separated the Up and Down goods lines from the Up and Down Local lines, thereby producing three pairs of tracks south of this point as far as Brent Sidings. North of Silkstream Junction there were just the Up and Down Fast and Slow lines. No. 42595 was allocated to Kentish Town from September 1956 having been at Chester since 1948.

The small signal box at Silkstream Junction was opened in 1890 to control the junction where the Down Local and Goods lines joined after the flyover. The original box was replaced by this one in 1924 and it was in operation until 1978. Fowler 2-6-4T No. 42335 was passing with an Up local on 2nd July 1958. It was allocated to St. Albans from December 1947 until November 1959 when it was transferred to Woodford Halse. No. 42335 returned to the Midland line at Kentish Town for a couple years from February 1960 until July 1962 when it moved to Rowsley along with two classmates and three Fairburns as many new BRC&W Type '2's arrived.

Probably on the same day as the previous picture, Johnson '3F' 0-6-0 No. 43474 runs tender-first with a southbound 'K' Class freight. Built by Neilson, Reid & Co. for the Midland Railway in 1896, it was in service until March 1961 and was at Bedford throughout the BR period.

Mill Hill Broadway

LM&SR 'Compound' 4-4-0 No. 41091 on a Down Ordinary Passenger train at Mill Hill Broadway in the early 1950s. The picture was taken while it was still allocated to Bedford; it moved to Leicester in January 1955. The station was originally 'Mill Hill' until September 1950 when the suffix 'Broadway' was added.

Fairburn 2-6-4T No. 42132 has just pulled out of Mill Hill Broadway with a Down local in the early 1950s. It was a BR-built engine, emerging from Derby Works in December 1949 and allocated to St. Albans where it stayed until February 1954 when it was transferred to Nottingham.

The Fairburn tank is so dirty the staff have chalked 2178 on the bunker of No. 42178 at Mill Hill Broadway on 22nd May 1957. It was built at Derby in November 1948 and arrived on the Midland Division from Chester in October 1956; it was at Kentish Town until February 1960.

No. 44564 with a southbound freight in the early 1950s was one of forty-five '4F' 0-6-0s built while William Stanier was Chief Mechanical Engineer of the LM&SR, entering service in July 1937. The LM&SR took an economic decision to order more of what was essentially the 1911 Midland Railway design when it needed additional medium sized freight locomotives, taking a type which had low running costs and avoiding the considerable expense of producing a completely new design. No. 44564 was allocated to Rowsley from before nationalisation until January 1960 when it went to Trafford Park.

'Crosti' boiler 2-10-0 No. 92026 with smoke emerging from the chimney on the side of the boiler at Mill Hill on 25th May 1957; the conventional chimney on the smokebox was only used when lighting up. No. 92026 entered traffic in June 1955 and was allocated to Wellingborough for the Brent coal traffic along with the other nine Crosti '9F's. The Crosti system was designed to obtain useful work from the large amount of heat lost through the chimney of an engine with a conventional boiler; on a '9F' this 'unused' energy was over 80% of that theoretically available from the burnt fuel. The hot gases from combustion, before expulsion, were passed through preheaters to raise boiler feed water temperature almost to boiling point under pressure; the heated water injected into the main boiler facilitated more efficient steam production than if the water came straight from the tender. The use of two pre-heaters, one on each side of the boiler as in the original Italian conversions was not possible on the '9F' because of the British loading gauge. Therefore, a single preheater was used which required the provision of a smaller boiler than on the standard '9F'. Numerous other design changes had to be made, including to the cylinders and reversing gear. The Crosti boiler engines were subject to numerous modifications over the next few years. Following reports of poor steaming, the draughting arrangement was redesigned and by the end of 1955 all ten engines were back at Crewe Works for this modification. At the same time, smoke deflector plates were fitted to the side chimney to reduce the amount of smoke entering the cab; this was partially successful. No. 92026 was converted from Crosti to conventional operation in September 1959.

The rather odd appearance of the Midland Railway 'ridge and furrow' station canopies at Mill Hill Broadway is evident in this view of a 'Jubilee' with a southbound express on the Up Fast on 22nd May 1957. A suburban train headed by a 2-6-4T waits in the Down Slow platform.

Driving Motor Brake Second No. M51635 is at the front of an eight-car DMU formed from two four-car sets departing from Mill Hill Broadway on a St. Pancras to St. Albans service on 23rd July 1960. Thirty of these Rolls-Royce powered four-car DMUs were built at Derby and became Class '127' under TOPS. They were high density sets with no gangway connections, and originally had seats for 352 Second Class passengers, later reduced when gangways were fitted. *C.R.L. Coles/Rail Archive Stephenson*

The 'furrow and ridge' canopies have gone and the Midland Railway buildings replaced by utilitarian brick and glass shelters but the signal box remains as a Class '127' DMU waits to depart with a St. Pancras service on 22nd February 1969. The station was rebuilt in 1967 when the M1 motorway was built literally feet away from the platforms (on the right of the picture). Note the lamps now bear the plain 'Mill Hill' although the name 'Mill Hill Broadway' was retained and is still in use today.

Elstree

Stanier 2-6-2T No. 40096 emerges from Elstree Tunnel with a Down stopping passenger train on 21st March 1953. It was built in 1935 and allocated to Kentish Town from October 1946 until January 1956, except for a few months at Ryecroft in mid-1952. The 1,058 yards long tunnel was on the boundary between Greater London and Hertfordshire. The Slow lines tunnel was built after the Fast lines bore.

On the same day, LM&SR-built 'Compound' 4-4-0 No. 41079 was working out its time on the Bedford Stoppers. It was at Bedford between November 1952 and May 1956, moving to Nottingham for its final six months in service,

'4F' 0-6-0 No. 44565 leaves Elstree New Tunnel with an Up goods train on 27th June 1953. It was one of the engines built in 1937 to what was essentially the Midland Railway Fowler design several years after Stanier became Chief Mechanical Engineer of the LM&SR. No. 44565 was at Rowsley from the end of 1950 until it was transferred to Trafford Park ten years later.

C.R.L. Coles/Rail Archive Stephenson

A Down express headed by 'Jubilee' No. 45725 *Repulse* approaching Elstree Station after passing through the tunnel in around 1950. It has British Railways L&NWR-style lined black livery with 8in. Gill Sans cab numbers and BRITISH RAILWAYS lettering on the tender; this was enthusiastically used by Crewe Works from August 1948 until July 1949 with forty-seven members of the class receiving the livery. *Repulse* was painted this way in December 1948 when it became No. 45725. It was transferred in October 1948 from Kentish Town to Sheffield Millhouses where it stayed until 1961. *Repulse* has an ex-'Royal Scot' No. 6157 'Old standard' 3,500 gallon tender which it had from new in September 1936 until January 1950.

An Up local train, probably from Bedford, departs behind BR Standard '4MT' 2-6-4T No. 80060 on 27th March 1954. A Down local is in the Down Slow platform. No. 80060 was new to Bedford in March 1953 and moved to Bury in January 1955 along with No. 80061. The name of the station has changed several times; it was originally 'Elstree' when opened in 1868 but changed to 'Elstree & Borehamwood' the following year. In 1904 it reverted to plain 'Elstree' but became 'Elstree & Borehamwood' again in September 1953, although this did not last, and it reverted to 'Elstree' in May 1974. It has operated as 'Elstree & Borehamwood' since 1988.

Fowler 2-6-4T No. 42342 ready to leave Elstree & Borehamwood with an Up local on 4th April 1959. It was transferred to its final shed, Kentish Town, in October 1958 and was withdrawn in June 1962. The covered footbridge was replaced by a plain steel open one soon after this picture was taken.

Stanier '8F' 2-8-0 No. 48195 approaching Elstree & Borehamwood station with one of the seemingly endless procession of coal trains from the East Midlands to Brent Sidings on 3rd October 1959. The LM&SR had been looking to replace the Midland Railway 0-6-0s with 2-8-0s on the coal trains to the Capital since 1923, the first year of the Grouping, but it was not until 1935 that the first 2-8-0s were built. Only 126 were in service when World War Two broke out, but after the design was selected for production during the war over 700 more were built within five years and most of these eventually found their way onto the London Midland Region. No. 48195 was built by the North British Locomotive Company in 1942 and was allocated to Toton from September 1950 until June 1962 when it was transferred to Westhouses.

Former Crosti-boilered '9F' 2-10-0 No. 92024 has just passed through Elstree & Borehamwood with a Toton to Brent coal train on 12th October 1963. In the background BRC&W Type '2' No. D5402 waits in the loop with a stopping goods that has called at the small yard. No. 92024 was then still at its original shed, Wellingborough, but was transferred to Kettering at the beginning of 1964. It had been converted from Crosti to conventional operation in early 1960. *Brian Stephenson*

On the same day, 'Peak' No. D95 heads the 12.3pm Sheffield Midland to St. Pancras express. It became No. 45054 under TOPS and was withdrawn in January 1985 after a traction motor flashover. It was due to be fitted with electric train heating in 1975 and become No. 45150 but was deemed unsuitable and the former No. D78 was substituted, which led to the highly unusual situation whereby both locomotives carried the number 45054 for two months. *Brian Stephenson*

Radlett

Running on the Down Slow line at Radlett, the 5.20pm St. Pancras - St. Albans behind Fowler 2-6-2T No. 40022 on 30th August 1958. It was built in December 1930 as LM&SR No. 15522 and was one of the forty built in 1930/1 fitted with condensing apparatus for working through the tunnels onto the Metropolitan Widened Lines in London. No. 40022 was allocated to St. Albans from July 1947 until February 1960; it was withdrawn from Cricklewood on 13th December 1962 – the last of the class.

Napsbury

Fairburn 2-6-4T No. 42156 with the 3.40pm St. Pancras to St. Albans leaving Napsbury on 30th August 1958. The station, which was of timber construction between two massive brick chimneys visible above the third coach, was opened in 1905 to serve the nearby hospital but was not well patronised and was closed on 14th September 1959. The signal box which controlled the Up Slow to Up Fast and Down Fast to Down Slow junctions lasted longer, until December 1979. No. 42156 was built at Derby after nationalisation, in June 1948, and had been at Low Moor, Stoke, Watford and Bangor before reaching Kentish Town in June 1956.

Two BR Sulzer Type '2's with No. D5211 leading No. D7574 on the Up Fast north of Radlett working a Saturday special, probably to the Motor Show at Earls Court, on 24th October 1964. The train is composed of LM&SR Stanier coaches; the 'T' headcode indicates an excursion or special train working within the LMR. Derby built No. D5211 was at Cricklewood from July 1963 until January 1965, became No. 25061 in May 1974 and was withdrawn in 1980. No. D7574 was one of the class built at Darlington, and was allocated to Cricklewood until March 1967. It stayed on the Midland lines until 1967 and then moved to the Birmingham, Liverpool and Manchester Divisions before going to the Western Region at Laira in October 1971. No. D7574 was renumbered to 25224 in February 1974 and moved back to the London Midland at Crewe in 1978 and was withdrawn there in 1986.

At the same location on the same day 'Peak' No. D162 is sandwiched between two brake tenders as it takes a lengthy coal train southwards. Even though what became the Class '46's under TOPS were mostly allocated to the North Eastern Region at this period a small number were based on the London Midland and were serviced at Toton. No. D162 was there until 1969 when it moved to the Western Region, becoming No. 46025 in February 1974. It was withdrawn for the first time in December 1980 but was reinstated and went to Gateshead where it was withdrawn again in April 1982 only to be reinstated until it finally succumbed in November 1984.

St. Albans

This train thundering through St.Albans City on the Up Fast is the 12.12pm Derby - St. Pancras, headed by BR Standard Caprotti Class '5' No. 73144 on 30th August 1958. It was at Leicester from new at the end of 1956 until March 1958 when it was transferred to Nottingham.

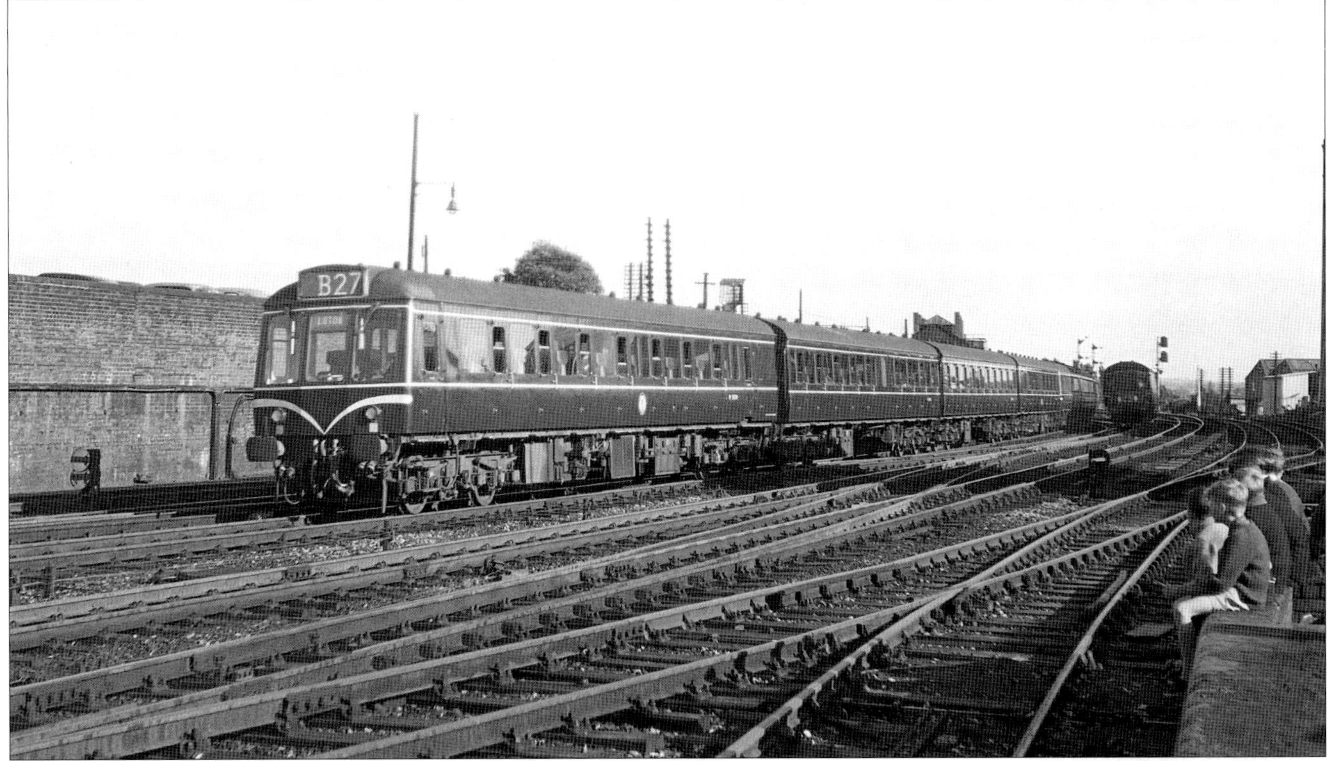

A group of spotters perched at the end of the bay platform at the south end of the station watch a Rolls-Royce-powered Derby-built DMU as it leaves St.Albans with a Luton-St. Pancras service on 14th July 1960. Motor Brake Second No. M51599 is nearest the camera and the set is passing the incoming DMU parcels van shown overleaf.

St. Albans shed is just visible as Gloucester Railway Carriage & Wagon Company Motor Parcels Van No. M55989 pulls into the station on 14th July 1960. These were introduced in 1959 and were powered by two AEC 230 bhp engines; they became Class '128' under TOPS and all were withdrawn by the end of 1990, No. M55989 going in 1982.

Hopefully those spotters will appreciate the glamour of the 'Midland Pullman' after the 'boring' DMUs as it passes through northwards on the same day. On the other hand, they may have been hoping for a 'Jubilee' or 'Royal Scot'.

7 – The North London Line

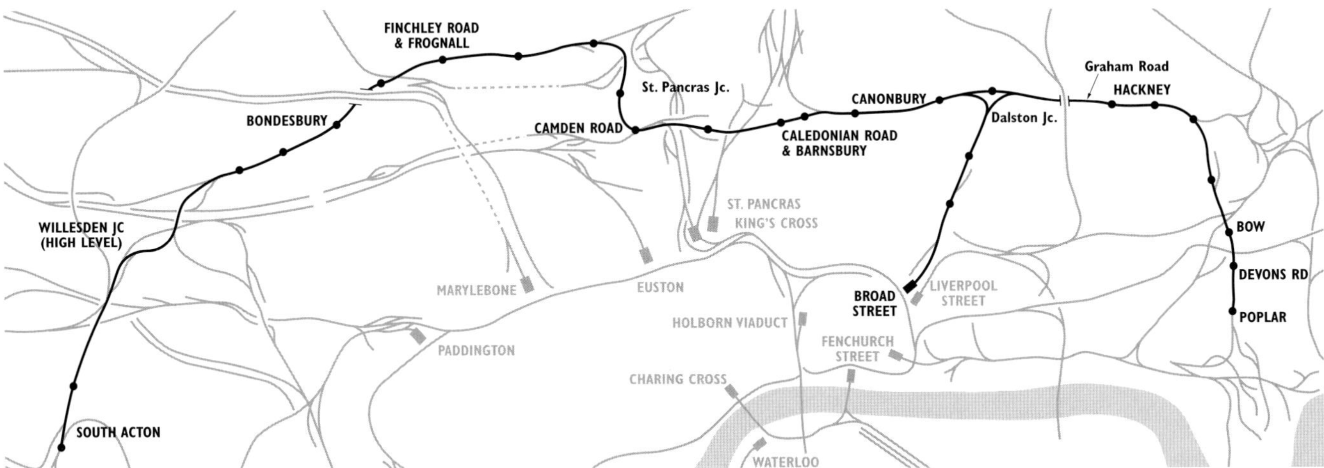

The North London Line had its origins in the East & West India Docks & Birmingham Junction Railway which provided a link for freight traffic from the L&NWR near Camden Town to the Blackwall dockland area at Stepney. Passenger traffic started in 1850 with a service from Islington to the London & Blackwall Railway's terminus at Fenchurch Street running over that company's tracks from a junction at Bow; services were soon extended to Camden Town and Hampstead Road. The unwieldy name was changed to the North London Railway in January 1853 and a line was completed in 1865 from Kingsland into a new City station at Broad Street, the traffic having quickly outgrown the shared station at Fenchurch Street. This work was mainly financed by the L&NWR which gained use of the line for its own services, opening a large goods station at Broad Street. The 'Premier Line' took over operation of the NLR in February 1909 having appointed two-thirds of the company's Directors for many years previously, although it remained an independent company until July 1922 when the L&NWR took it over completely.

From 1860, North London Railway trains worked over the Hampstead Junction Railway, which left the NLR just west of Camden Town through to a connection with the L&NWR at Willesden Junction. It was managed by the NLR from 1864 and was taken over by the L&NWR in 1867. From Willesden, trains continued to Kew over the North & South Western Junction Railway. In 1911 the L&NWR approved an electrification programme for its suburban lines which would include the route from Broad Street to Kew and Richmond (the Richmond Extension Line from Kew was completed in 1869). This was completed in 1916, with peak-hour workings to Watford via the Hampstead Junction introduced the following year. An all-day service to Watford on the more direct route via Chalk Farm (renamed as Primrose Hill in 1950) began in 1922. Little changed until the Second World War, apart from the introduction of new rolling stock in the late 1920s. However, the line suffered severely from wartime bombing, especially in the East End of London, and the passenger service to Poplar, which had started in 1866 over the former goods lines from Bow, was permanently discontinued in May 1944.

There was a limited amount of modernisation of the Broad Street facilities in 1957; the main station building was closed and replaced by two small buildings on the concourse and the refreshment room was privatised. The Beeching Report in 1963 proposed closure of the remaining section of the North London line but, fortunately, strenuous local opposition reversed this. However, moves to close Broad Street station began in 1979 with the aim of transferring the NLR trains to Liverpool Street. Trains to Richmond would run from North Woolwich via Kingsland and Stratford Low Level over a line to be electrified. This service did not start until 1985, leaving Broad Street, which had become increasingly decrepit, with only a few peak-hour trains to Watford; demolition actually started in 1985 and it was finally closed in June 1986.Today, the only part of the North London line that has not been re-opened is between Victoria Park and Bow. It forms an important part of the London Overground and the Docklands Light Railway runs over the old route between Poplar and Bow.

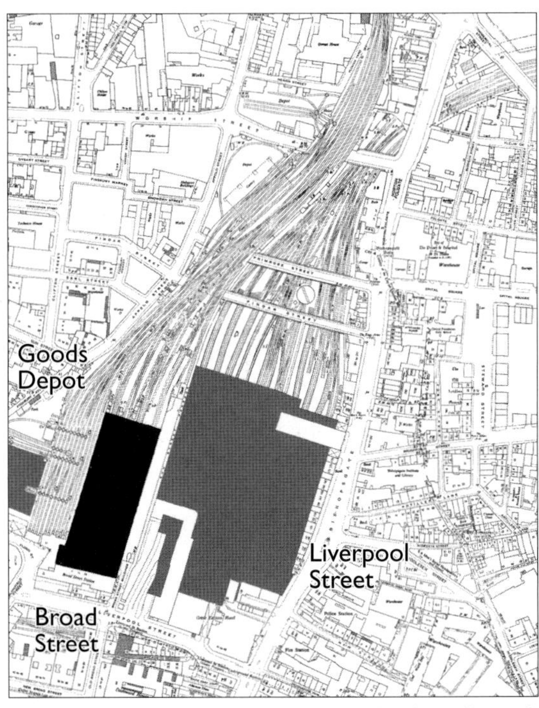

Broad Street station was literally next to the Great Eastern's Liverpool Street station.

Broad Street

The station building which opened in 1865 was constructed using white Suffolk bricks, with decorative Portland stone, terracotta and Peterhead granite. The central clock tower was 75ft high. The Portland stone façade was added in 1913 and incorporated an entrance to the Central Line tube which had been opened a year earlier. The external staircase on the right in this 12th May 1961 picture was carefully dismantled during the station's demolition and stored for possible use elsewhere.

The signalman watches North London Railway 0-6-0T No. 58859 as it reverses into Broad Street station before working the LCGB 'Poplar & Edgware' rail tour on 5th May 1956. It took the train to Poplar, handing over to 'Jinty' No. 47484. No. 58859 returned the party to Broad Street from Canonbury, taking over the train from 'N2' 0-6-2T No. 69506. Thirty of these 0-6-0Ts were built by the North London Railway between 1879 and 1905, and fifteen survived into BR days. In the background is Broad Street No. 1 signal box that stood at the end of Platforms 2 and 3; it dated back to the 1891 rearrangement and controlled the NLR platforms. In the background is an Ivatt Class '4' 2-6-0 in the yard of Broad Street goods depot. *C.R.L. Coles/Rail Archive Stephenson*

The almost deserted interior of Broad Street in 1959 with the full 457ft long overall roof still in place; this was designed by the L&NWR Chief Engineer William Baker and had two 95ft spans supported in the centre by cast ornamental columns. It was cut right back for safety reasons in 1967/68. DMUs worked to Stevenage and Hitchin from 1959 until the service ceased in November 1976.

Fairburn 2-6-4T No. 42099 departs with a Watford service on 17th July 1960. It was a Southern Region engine until December 1959 when it was transferred from Ashford to Watford. On the left, obscured by the train, was a large goods depot, opened by the L&NWR in 1868.

The Cravens Class '105' DMUs worked the suburban services out of Kings Cross from late 1958 and into Broad Street via the Canonbury spur. Driving Trailer Composite No. E56456 was waiting there in the early 1970s while on the right was a Class '501' EMU working to either Watford or Richmond. In front of the DMU is Broad Street No. 2 signal box built in 1876 which worked the L&NWR platforms on the west side of the station. It outlived the newer No. 1 box which was closed in November 1969 when the station layout was rationalised and the tracks on the eastern side which had served the line to Poplar, which was never electrified and closed to passenger services in 1944, were removed. Platforms 1, 2, 3 and 9 were taken out of use and Platform 4 followed suit in 1976.

The photographer has managed to leave his bag in the picture as he records Class '501' EMU Motor Open Brake Second No. M61150 arriving on a Richmond service as denoted by the 'B4' headcode. The units were in all-over blue with full yellow ends from the late 1960s and worked until 1985 when they were replaced by Class '313's transferred from the Great Northern line and SR '2-EPB' units. During this period they almost always worked in fixed sets: Motor Open Brake Second No. M61150 working with Trailer Second No. M70150 and Driving Trailer Open Brake Second No. M75150.

Class '501' Driving Trailer Open Brake Second No. M75160 is at the front of a Watford service, coded 'B2'. The train shed roof was cut-back in 1967/8 after it became unsafe and to reduce maintenance costs. In the background is the distinctive outline of the National Westminster Tower at 25 Old Broad Street under construction. In plan view it was shaped like the Nat West logo of three chevrons arranged hexagonally. At 600ft high, it was the tallest building in the UK until 1990 when One Canary Wharf was completed and it was the first sky-scraper in the City of London; it remained the tallest there until 2009. Construction began in 1971 and the Tower was topped out in 1977; Nat West sold it in 1997 and it is now named 'Tower 42', after its forty-two cantilevered floors.

Bow Works and Devons Road shed

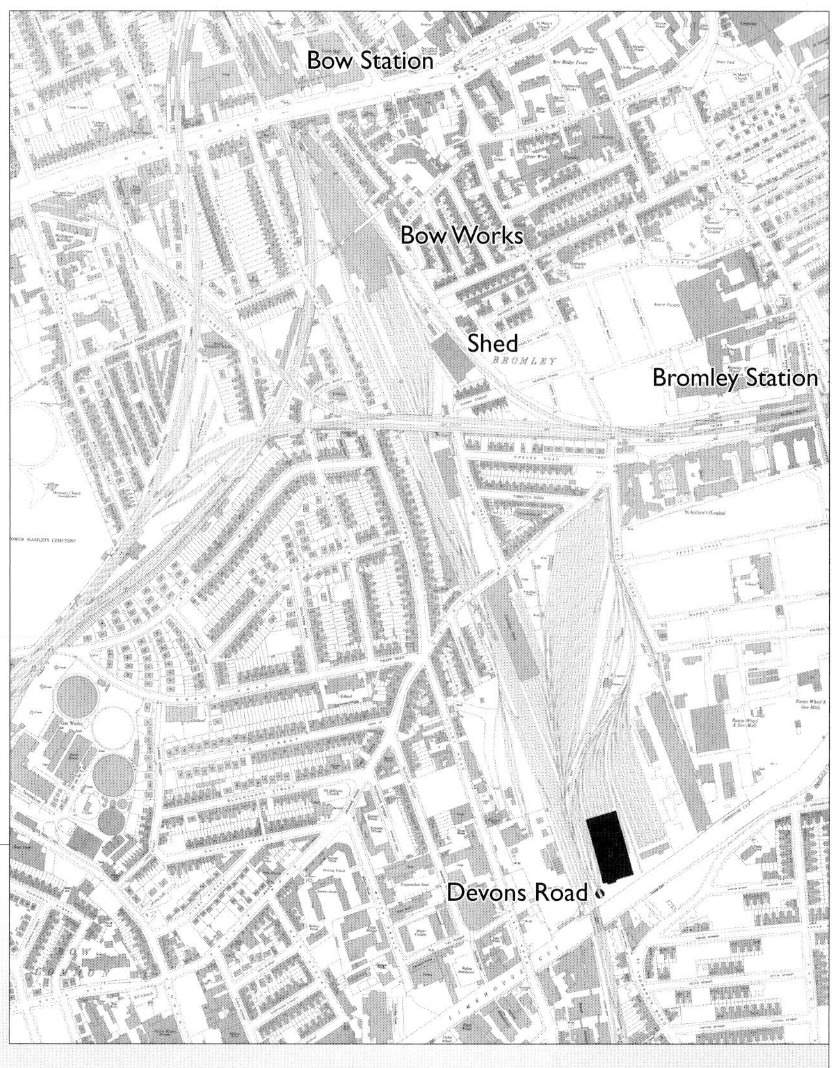

The North London Railway had only one motive power depot, opened at Bow around 1850; it was demolished in 1882 and the site used to enlarge the Works there. It was replaced by two ten-road northlight roof sheds of L&NWR design built nearby at Devons Road. In 1935, No. 2 shed was deemed surplus to requirements by the LM&SR and was demolished, and at the same date a new concrete mechanical coaling plant was installed. No. 1 shed was badly damaged by bombing during the Second World War and it was rebuilt with a new louvred roof in 1946.

Devons Road was converted into the first dedicated diesel maintenance depot by British Railways in 1958. At this date it had an allocation of forty-one locomotives and the last of these, '3F' 0-6-0T No. 47517, left in August. They were to be replaced by thirty-three diesels: fifteen of 1,000 hp, ten of 800 hp and eight shunters. However, the diesel depot had a short life because of changing operating patterns and declining freight traffic. It was closed in February 1964 and its remaining diesel locomotives transferred to Stratford. Devons Road was Coded 13B from 1935 grouped with the former LT&S sheds until the latter were transferred to the Eastern Region in 1949; it remained with the London Midland Region and became 1D and finally 1J in September 1963.

Two blocks of flats built in the mid-1950s overlooked the depot and this view on 11th August 1957 clearly shows the layout with the tracks which were formerly covered by No. 2 shed on the left of No. 1 shed. Three of the four engine types which were on the shed's books during the 1950s are visible: from left to right a North London Railway tank, a '3F' 0-6-0T and a '4F' in front of the shed; the one missing class is the Ivatt '4MT' 2-6-0.

Bow Works was a cramped and difficult to photograph works and there are very few pictures of locomotives standing outside. However, there was a little known and rarely photographed two-road engine shed in the south east corner of the Works complex. Fairburn 2-6-4T No. 42231 from Neasden had visited Bow Works for Casual Damage Repairs from 3rd February until 9th March 1959 while Stanier 2-6-4T No. 42520, just visible on the left, made a one day visit to the Works on 16th March 1959 after being released from 'Heavy Intermediate' overhaul at Derby Works. Engine History Cards show that engines returning to the LT&S from Derby Works usually spent one day in Bow Works on their way back. Bow Works closed at the end of 1959.

Former North London Railway 0-6-0T No. 58859 displaying Target code 41 at Devons Road on 8th October 1955. These short wheelbase, outside-cylindered tank engines were particularly suited for operation over the numerous dock lines in the Poplar district of London but were less appropriate when working local freight trains on the main line. Built at Bow Works in 1889, No. 58859 was allocated to Devons Road from March 1949 until withdrawn in October 1957. No. 58859 and its classmates were not fitted with BR smokebox number plates; this applied to most of the engines repaired only at Bow Works, including those from the LT&S sheds.

Ivatt Class '4' 2-6-0 No. 43001 on 16th April 1955; it is ten years after the war ended and they are only just building the replacement new flats. It still has the hideous and ineffective double chimney that the first thirty of the class were built with; this was replaced by a single chimney and revised draughting arrangements in August 1956. No. 43001 was at Devons Road from January 1951 until October 1957 when it was transferred to Nuneaton. Devons Road also had Nos 43000, 43020-43022 and 43024 over the same period; they were used on cross-London freight duties along the North London Line to the Southern marshalling yards at Feltham and Hither Green until displaced by the Type '1' diesels. The white-washed wall on the right was the rear wall of No. 2 shed which backed on to the Limehouse Cut linking the Thames with the River Lea.

Left: Fresh out of Bow Works in around 1955, ex-Midland Railway '2F' 0-6-0 No. 58215 from Kentish Town where it was allocated until May 1956 when it was transferred to Bedford. Built by Beyer, Peacock in 1883 No. 58215 was in service for almost eighty years, lasting until March 1961. The new concrete louvred roof of No. 1 shed dating from 1946 shows up well.

Right: In addition to the complement of fifteen English Electric 1,000bhp Type '1's, Devons Road had an initial batch of ten BTH 800bhp Type '1's, Nos D8200-D8209. These were transferred to the Eastern Region at the end of 1959 and replaced by the English Electric design. No. D8203 and its classmates were all withdrawn before they received their Class '15' TOPS numbers. However, it was not scrapped and was converted to an unpowered Carriage Heating unit, transferred to Departmental Stock and renumbered to DB 968003 in November 1969 before finally succumbing in July 1981.

The first twenty English Electric Type '1' 1,000 bhp Bo-Bos delivered from Vulcan Foundry between June 1957 and March 1958 were originally allocated to Devons Road, primarily for cross-London transfer freight work over the North London line. They were fitted with Hudd ATC equipment for operation over the LT&S. Nos D8000-D8004 were transferred to Crewe South in late 1958 leaving fifteen at Devons Road. Then ten of the class ordered for the Eastern Region GER lines and delivered in late 1959, Nos D8035-D8044, were instead sent to Devons Road in exchange for the depot's ten BTH Type '1's Nos D8200-D8209 thus making all of the Type '1's at Devons Road a single class. No. D8008 on shed with No. D8009 in 1959 was at Devons Road from October 1957 until February 1964 when the shed closed and it went with its classmates to Willesden, where it stayed until April 1969 when all those still at that depot were transferred to the Nottingham Division. It subsequently worked on the Scottish and Eastern Regions and was withdrawn from Thornaby in February 1989. In the background is No. D2902, an 0-4-0 diesel-hydraulic of 330bhp built by the North British Locomotive Company. The first eight of the fourteen in this class went to Devons Road, as replacements for the steam tank engines. No. D2902 went into traffic in April 1958 and was there until February 1964 when it was transferred to Stratford along with Nos D2900-D2906; its final move was as a works shunter to Crewe Works in April 1966 and it was withdrawn there in February 1967.

The North London Line

Graham Road

Graham Road was east of Dalston Junction on the original NLR line through Hackney, Bow and Bromley to Poplar. The passenger service to Poplar ceased in May 1944. In 1854 the Eastern Counties Railway, later the Great Eastern Railway, built a line from Stratford via Hackney Wick to a junction with the NLR at Victoria Park, which was between Hackney and Bow. This facilitated significant cross-London freight traffic through to Stratford and brought engines from three of the 'Big Four' companies to the line, the ex-Great Western engines were prohibited because of their greater width over the cylinders.

'WD' 2-8-0 No. 90169 passes Graham Road signal box running towards Hackney Station with an eastbound coal train on 1st November 1958. It was built by the North British Locomotive Company as WD No. 7186 and became BR No. 90169 in February 1950; it was allocated to New England shed at Peterborough from September 1948 until June 1962. *K.L. Cook/Rail Archive Stephenson*

'N2' 0-6-2T No. 69552 approaches Graham Road signal box heading a westbound transfer freight with insulated meat containers at the front of the train, on 1st November 1958. It was built for the L&NER by Beyer, Peacock in 1925 and was at Hornsey from July 1957 until three weeks after this picture was taken, when it was transferred to Grantham. Lorries owned by H. & H. Bristow Ltd, 'The Eastern Counties Delivery Service', which line the adjacent Cottrill Road are in all four of the pictures taken from this viewpoint.
K.L. Cook/Rail Archive Stephenson

Diesels began to take over the transfer freights over the North London line from the end of 1957. On the same November day as the pictures on the previous page, English Electric Type '1' No. D8019 works an eastbound transfer freight. It was built in March 1958 and was at Devons Road until February 1964 when the shed closed and it was transferred to Stratford. It subsequently moved many times, working on the Eastern and Scottish Regions before being withdrawn as No. 20019 for the first time in November 1983. It was reinstated to Toton in 1985 and was in service until October 1991.

K.L. Cook/Rail Archive Stephenson

One of the former Devons Road '3F' 0-6-0Ts replaced by Type '1' diesels in 1958, Camden's No. 47514 approaches Graham Road signal box with a westbound transfer freight on 21st March 1959. The small seven-road coal depot in the foreground, and which was still in use at this date, was accessed from a loop off the line on which the train is running; it closed in October 1965. *K.L. Cook/Rail Archive Stephenson*

Another example of the wide variety of locomotive types which could be seen over this section of the North London line; only ex-Great Western types were prohibited because of the greater width over their cylinders. Bulleid 'Q1' 0-6-0 No. 33013 from Feltham shed has just passed under the Great Eastern Cambridge line near Graham Road with a transfer freight to Feltham on 21st March 1959, as an 'N7' 0-6-2T crosses over the bridge with a suburban train from Liverpool Street. Hackney Downs Junction station was immediately in front of the 'N7'. *T.G. Hepburn/Rail Archive Stephenson*

Canonbury

English Electric Type '1' No. D8011 passes through Canonbury on 16th May 1963. Delivered to Devons Road in November 1957, it went to Willesden when the shed closed in February 1964. After spells at Toton, Eastfield, Tinsley and Immingham it was withdrawn as No. 20011 in February 1987. Canonbury was the second station west after Mildmay Park when the North London Railway split at Dalston Junction; the station buildings were demolished in June 1969 and rebuilding was completed in 1970. The link to the former Great Northern Railway Main Line at Finsbury Park, opened in 1874, left the North London Railway shortly after Canonbury.

Caledonian Road & Barnsbury

One of Devons Road's '3F' 0-6-0Ts, Vulcan Foundry-built No. 47488, passes through Caledonian Road & Barnsbury on 17th August 1957. It was there from before nationalisation until ousted by the new diesels in November 1957 and transferred to Edge Hill; it stayed at the Liverpool shed until withdrawn in late 1962. The station was opened in 1870 as 'Barnsbury' and became 'Caledonian Road & Barnsbury' in 1893. The 'Jinty' is on the non-electrified side of the station which became disused in the early 1960s. Someone appears to be growing potatoes on the platform.

Stanier 2-6-4T No. 42616 on the electrified side of Caledonian Road & Barnsbury station with a westbound train in September 1963. North British Locomotive Company built in 1937, No. 42616 was at Watford from September 1961 until 1965 and had been fitted with the AWS needed for operation in the London area during February 1962. It ended its days on the North Eastern Region, at Low Moor from May 1967 until withdrawn in September.

St. Pancras Junction

An unidentified '3F' 0-6-0T makes its way Light Engine westwards over the bridge which crossed over the Midland Main Line on 13th October 1956. There was a connection on the left after the signal box which curved down to St. Pancras goods depot. The view from below the bridge is shown on page 116 in Chapter 6.

Camden Road

Two LM&SR-built Euston-Watford EMUs arrive at Camden Road station on a Watford to Broad Street service in 1963. They are in plain green livery with small yellow warning panels. The tracks divided here beyond the signal box: left to Primrose Hill to meet the L&NWR line out of Euston almost opposite Camden shed, and right over the line built by the Hampstead Junction Railway to Kentish Town West, Gospel Oak and then Willesden High Level. The station was renamed Camden Road in September 1950; it was previously known as Camden Town. *Kenneth Field/Rail Archive Stephenson*

Finchley Road & Frognal

'J19' 0-6-0 No. 64657 from Stratford shed approaching Finchley Road & Frognal station with an eastbound freight from the Southern Region on 7th May 1955. The 'J19' was a Gresley rebuild of ex-Great Eastern Railway engines with the larger boilers as used on the 'D16/3' 4-4-0s, with a round-topped firebox in place of the original Belpaire type and larger cabs.

Brondesbury

The English Electric Type '1' diesels virtually monopolised the North London freight traffic in the early 1960s. No. D8010 runs through Brondesbury with a train comprising mostly insulated containers on 3rd October 1960; the disc code indicates a freight between the Eastern Region and Hither Green. No. D8010 was delivered to Devons Road in November 1957, moving to Willesden when the shed closed in February 1964. After spells at Toton, Haymarket, Eastfield, Tinsley and Immingham it was withdrawn from Toton as No. 20010 in December 1991.

Willesden Junction High Level

A BR built three-car EMU leaves Willesden Junction High Level on a Broad Street to Richmond service on 16th March 1963. The Richmond service was one of the few in London marked for the Beeching Axe in 1963 but strenuous opposition to closure by local authorities along the route brought a reprieve in 1965, and of course it is now part of the 'London Overground'. *Brian Stephenson*

Below: On the same day, Brush Type '2' No. D5513 passes through the High Level station with a Temple Mills to Feltham transfer freight which will travel via Kensington Olympia and Clapham Junction. One of the first batch of the class delivered to the Eastern Region in 1958, No. D5513 was always allocated to Stratford shed up until withdrawal as No. 31013 in 1979. It was transferred to Departmental stock as a Train Heating Unit, renumbered ADB968013, and was in use until 1983. The first four wagons in the train were all the subject of Airfix plastic model kits in the 1960s; at the front are three 'Presflo' cement wagons followed by an 'Esso' 35 ton Class 'B' oil tanker which carried fuel oil, diesel oil, or kerosene.

A sole passenger waits for his train at a typical run-down 1970s Willesden Junction. The picture is taken looking southwards; immediately after the signal box was a junction with the left-hand fork to the West London line through Kensington (Olympia) to Clapham Junction and the right to Acton, Kew and Richmond.

South Acton

One of the LM&SR-built 3-car 'GEC' EMUs calls at South Acton on a Richmond to Broad Street service in the mid-1950s. Unlike the earlier 'Oerlikon' units these had compartments with slam doors at each bay; the motor coach with its three prominent cooling vents on each side leads. The service to Kew and Richmond had been operated by electric units since October 1916. The wooden platforms at the station were still in use right up until 1986.
Brian Stephenson

8 – The London, Tilbury & Southend

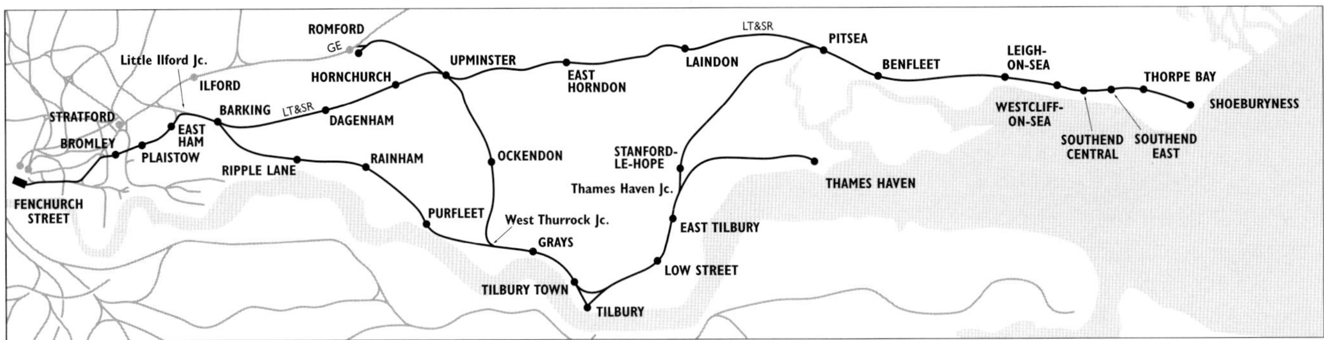

The LT&SR became an independent company in 1862, having previously been jointly-owned by the Eastern Counties Railway and the London & Blackwall Railway (both later part of the Great Eastern Railway) in an unorthodox arrangement the details of which are outside the scope of this book. The line to Tilbury was opened in 1854 and extended to Southend in 1856. At the eastern end, access to London was gained via the ECR at Stratford and the L&BR to the latter's Fenchurch Street station. There were complex leasing and financial arrangements and the LT&SR did not take over the full management of the line until 1875; this included the purchase of its own locomotives and rolling stock. The most important development at the end of the nineteenth century was the building of the 'Southend Direct' line between Barking and Pitsea, opened in 1888, partly in response to the building of new docks at Tilbury. It was thought that the original route via Tilbury would not be able to accommodate the Southend traffic and the additional traffic generated from the docks. Other new works undertaken in this period were an extension of the line from Southend to Shoeburyness and a branch from Romford to Grays via Upminster.

In the first decade of the twentieth century the LT&SR was the subject of a possible takeover by the Great Eastern Railway which made an initial offer in 1900 that was rejected as too low. There were further discussions in 1905 but nothing happened until 1910 when both the Midland Railway and the North London Railway, on behalf of the L&NWR made approaches. By this date the traffic on the Southend line had increased to such an extent that the LT&SR was faced with significant capital expenditure, including electrification for which it already had powers. The attraction for the Midland was the opportunity to tap into the major expansion at Tilbury Docks and they moved quickly and very much 'under the radar' to agree a deal with the LT&SR General Manager in January 1911. The GER had been caught off-guard and were naturally not happy. The takeover had to gain Parliamentary approval, which proved to be a protracted affair, and this was not given until August 1912; the takeover was backdated to 1st January of that year. The Act included arrangements for the continuing use of Fenchurch Street station and a requirement to electrify the line to Southend within seven years. The most obvious indication of the takeover was the repainting of the passenger engines in crimson lake and the goods engines in black; also, their names were removed and they were renumbered.

The outbreak of the First World War and its aftermath prevented any major changes during the Midland regime. The Whitelegg

Fenchurch Street

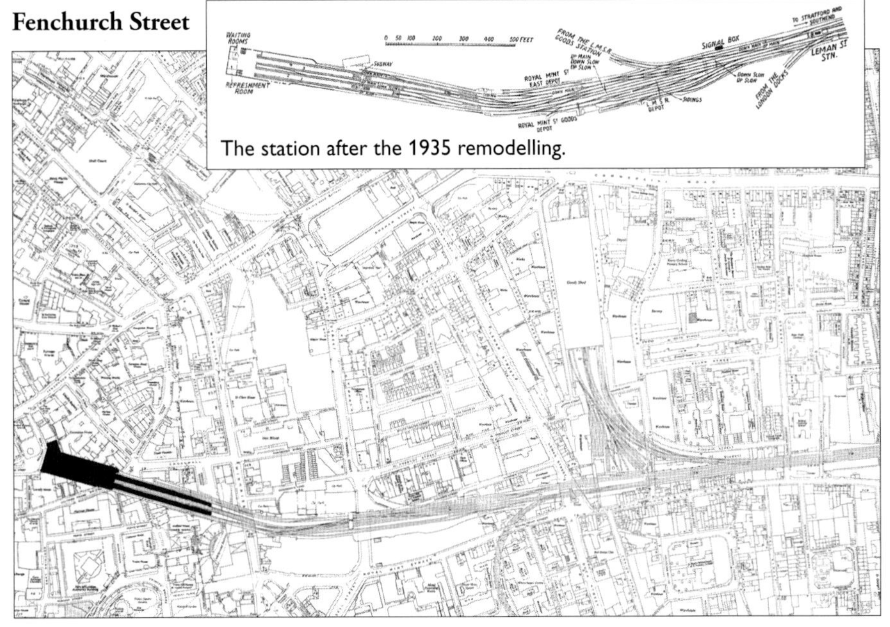

The station after the 1935 remodelling.

Fenchurch Street was the first station in the City of London when it was opened in 1841 by the London & Blackwall Railway. It was enlarged in 1854 for the newly formed LT&SR. In 1862 the Great Eastern Railway took over the L&BR and Fenchurch Street became the company's suburban line terminus, until Liverpool Street opened in 1874. Traffic on the LT&SR steadily increased until it was acquired by the Midland Railway in 1912. The station came under the L&NER at the 1923 Grouping but by then the LT&S services of the LM&SR considerably overshadowed those of its owners. However, a major remodelling of the station was completed in April 1935 with rearrangement of the approach lines, lengthening of the platforms and improved amenities. The LM&SR contributed two-thirds of the cost. The L&NER services to North Woolwich ended in 1940 and those to Loughton in 1947. The remaining former GER Ilford line trains stopped using the station when the Liverpool Street to Shenfield electrification was completed in November 1949.

4-4-2Ts continued to handle the passenger traffic and although a 2-6-4T design was sketched out at Derby in 1914, no new engines were ordered until after the 1923 Grouping when more 4-4-2Ts appeared. The Midland did however invest in new rolling stock, building 127 coaches between 1913 and 1923. It was left to the LM&SR to undertake major capital expenditure under what was termed the 'Southend Scheme', quadrupling the Barking-Upminster section and improving the layout and facilities at many stations including Fenchurch Street. New stations were built at Chalkwell and Leigh-on-Sea, at Shoeburyness the shed was modernised and additional carriage sidings were provided. In 1934 the line finally received more powerful motive power when thirty-seven Stanier three-cylinder 2-6-4Ts were introduced and an improved peak-hour timetable came into effect in April 1935. Seventeen new eleven-coach non-corridor sets were built, and eight sets were made up from Midland built stock transferred in.

After nationalisation in 1948, the LT&S came under control of the Eastern Region from February 1949 although the locomotive stock was not officially transferred until April 1953. The 'Tilbury' became known as the 'Misery Line' during the 1950s as punctuality declined because of staff shortages, especially locomotive maintenance men. Peak-hour trains were frequently cancelled, and vociferous commuters ensured much negative press coverage. Electrification was on the agenda from 1949 but precedence was given to the GER Shenfield line and work did not begin until 1960, although a number of interim track and station improvements were carried out between 1954 and 1957. The last of the LT&SR-built coaches were finally taken out of service in early 1956, seventy having survived until the Eastern Region took over. To replace these, six four-coach sets were built in 1953 using new bodies on underframes from withdrawn GE Shenfield line coaches and thirty new BR standard compartment coaches followed in 1954. The number of 2-6-4Ts was increased with more Fairburn tanks to add to those built in 1946/7 and then three batches of BR standards arrived between 1953 and 1957, eliminating the few remaining 4-4-2Ts by the end of 1958. Although electric operation of off-peak services began in November 1961 it was not until June 1962 that steam traction finally ceased, twenty of the new EMUs having to be transferred to the Great Eastern section in January to replace faulty units on that line, and they did not return until February and March.

The electrified lines on the right are the 1,500Volt DC system which was for a planned shuttle service between Fenchurch Street and a new interchange bay at Stratford. Platforms 1 and 2 and all four approach tracks were provided with catenary, but the project was abandoned, although empty electric trains ran under the wires from time to time to keep them clean for emergency use. They would be converted later to 6.25kV/25kV AC operation and in November 1961 the first electric trains began running on the newly electrified LT&SR, to steam timings in off-peak hours. Note the inspection pit for the steam engines awaiting their next duty.

Above: Platforms 1 and 2 at Fenchurch Street, which had formerly been used by the Great Eastern line trains to Loughton and Ilford, were taken over by LT&S services to Tilbury in November 1949. The steam trains operated under the abortive 1,500 Volt DC wires at Fenchurch Street throughout the 1950s.

Above: Fairburn No. 42226 after arrival at Fenchurch Street on 24th January 1959. It was built at Derby in May 1946 and was one of ten delivered to the LT&S, followed by another ten in 1947 and eight more in 1948/9. No. 42226 would remain at Plaistow until the end of LT&S steam in June 1962 when it was transferred to Stoke, from where it was withdrawn in June 1964.

The Fairburn 2-6-4Ts were followed by an influx of BR Standard 2-6-4Ts, twelve in 1953/4, ten in 1954/5 and a final six in 1956. This brought the total LT&S complement of Class '4' tanks for the final years of steam up to eighty-one, compared with only thirty-seven in the late 1930s. This both illustrated the growth of traffic and the inability of British Railways to concentrate classes together in areas to aid maintenance. No. 80098, resting at Fenchurch Street on 4th April 1959, went new to Plaistow in September 1954, moving to Tilbury in October 1959 when that shed was officially closed.

Stanier 2-6-4T No. 42522 stands in Platform 1 with a short parcels train on 22nd August 1960. The three-cylinder tanks were designed specifically for the LT&S commuter service when introduced as part of the LM&SR 1930s Southend Line improvements. There were weight restrictions on the L&NER-owned section of the route into Fenchurch Street from Gas Factory Junction, Bow which was carried on numerous brick arches through the built-up area of inner East London. A Fowler 2-6-4T had been at Plaistow for trials in early 1933 but it appears that it proved unacceptable to the L&NER Civil Engineer. The extra complication of three-cylinder propulsion was attributed at the time of their introduction to the need for better balancing to permit their use over this section. However, it is likely that the need for rapid acceleration away from the line's many stops was another reason for their design. At nationalisation, most of the three-cylinder engines were allocated to Shoeburyness, and all of them were there by 1956. They were principally used on services on the direct line via Upminster working the peak-hour business trains. One of the few changes made at Fenchurch Street prior to the LT&S electrification was the provision in 1953 of fluorescent lighting with the unusual, possibly unique, flying-saucer shaped diffusers. On the one above No. 42522 the bottom half has fallen away – perhaps that is why the design was not rolled out! In the background is the 'Fenchurch Buffet', part of a combined cafeteria, buffet and waiting-room built across the concourse in the 1930s modernisation. Note the large board at the end of the platform advertising Underwoods' service which developed and printed films on the 'Same Day'.

The first of the three-cylinder tanks built with a modified bunker having tapered/sloping rather than parallel sides, No. 42508 backs into the station on 28th February 1959. The signal box spanning the tracks in the left background was built in 1935 when three-aspect colour lights and electric point motors were installed as part of the modernisation work at Fenchurch Street. The expenditure enabled a significant increase in the peak-hour services, twenty-two Up on the Southend line and six Up on the Tilbury line compared with sixteen and three; there was a similar increase for the Down services. To accommodate these further down the line, 'Skip-stopping' had to be used for stations between Upminster and Shoeburyness.

Stanier three-cylinder 2-6-4T No. 42528 approaching Fenchurch Street 'under the wires' with a train from Southend in 1962. Most services on the LT&S were classified as Class '2' stopping passenger trains but the hourly service on the direct line via Upminster ran under Class '1' headlamps. Limited electric services began running into Fenchurch Street in November 1961, but it was not until June 1962 that steam traction was finally eliminated.

Stanier 2-6-4T No. 42520 departing with a Saturday peak hour train on 16th May 1959 with Fairburn No. 42224 peeping out on the right of the picture. Although many more modern carriages appeared during the 1950s, the most common stock on the Fenchurch Street-Shoeburyness trains were the 1920s-vintage LM&SR-built wooden-bodied carriages, although in this instance the third vehicle is a 1934 LM&SR steel-bodied suburban coach. Note the nice example of a stacked three-route ground signal, probably of L&NER design, and the train retarder on the right-hand running rail in the centre of the photograph.

Bow – Gas Factory Junction

Stanier 2-6-4T No. 42519 passes Gas Factory Junction signal box with a train for Fenchurch Street on 13th June 1959, where the line to Stratford joins the main LT&SR Main Line, and the train is passing over this junction. Until 1858 when a new line was opened between Gas Factory Junction and Barking the LT&SR trains had to travel via Stratford to reach Fenchurch Street. The track immediately to the right of No. 42519 is a line down to the local coal and goods yard, and that to the right of the hut is a spur from the North London Railway Poplar line. The viaduct visible in the background is part of the forty-one-arch structure from Gas Factory Junction to Campbell Road Junction near Bromley and forms part of the 1858 New Line. Note the overhead equipment which was an extension of the 1,500 Volt DC electrification used on the Liverpool Street-Shenfield line.

Bromley

Approaching Bromley from Campbell Road Junction with a Down train, Stanier 2-6-4T No. 42526 on 26th August 1956. The engines from No. 42525 onwards had cabs with a half-height door and a semi-circular cut-out at head level immediately behind the door opening. Campbell Road signal box is in the distance beyond the two bridges which crossed over the North London line. This section of line, between Campbell Road and East Ham, was quadrupled between 1902 and 1905, and the District Line tracks on the right were electrified.

Above: Only a few main-line trains called at Bromley after 1940 and they ceased completely after electrification in 1962. Stanier 2-6-4T No. 42511 passes through with a Down train of Midland Railway built LT&S stock on 26th August 1956. The station was renamed 'Bromley-by-Bow' in May 1967 and was transferred from British Railways to London Transport on 1st January 1969. The District Line tracks are on the left; these were completely separated from the BR tracks in 1962. The large building on the right was part of St. Andrews Hospital.

Left: Fairburn 2-6-4T No. 42684 with a Down train from Fenchurch Street on 26th August 1956. Note the two Hudd ATC ramps on the Up track. The system used magnetic induction and the inductors were positioned around fifteen yards apart and around 200 yards from the distant signal they were protecting. The first was a permanent magnet and the second an electro-magnet which was energised only when the signal was pulled off thus producing a fail-safe mechanism. The engines were fitted with a receiver which detected the magnetic fields from the inductors. If the distant was at clear, the first inductor opened the receiver and the second one closed it. If it was at caution, the receiver remained open and an indicator in the cab gave a warning and a horn was sounded.

From 1948 only Hudd ATC-fitted engines could work over the LT&S which restricted the choice of engines to work excursion trains onto the line. Hughes-Fowler 'Crab' 2-6-0 No. 42870 heads a returning excursion through Bromley on 26th August 1956. The W708 reporting number indicates a train for the Western Division – the paper numbers were only carried on Bank Holiday weekends. No. 42870 was built as LM&SR No. 13170 at Crewe in May 1930 and was renumbered as 2870 in 1935. It was allocated to Willesden from May 1947 until March 1962 when it went to Nuneaton; its ATC equipment was fitted in November 1947.

Brush Type '2' diesels allocated to Stratford but based at Ripple Lane replaced the Whitelegg 0-6-2Ts on LT&S freight work. No. D5517 heads a short freight on the Up through line at the west end of Bromley Station on 12th May 1961. No. D5517 was at Stratford from new in September 1958 until October 1967 and was withdrawn in 1980 as No. 31017. It has passed the 1905 built signal box which was still in use at this date, although colour light signals had replaced the LT&SR mechanical signals as part of the electrification project. The large sign at the platform end in front of the box read 'Way out to Devons Road and St. Andrews Hospital'. The post-war flats on the right were built where the Workhouse had been situated.

Plaistow Shed

The main shed of the LT&SR was situated on the south side of the line between West Ham and Plaistow stations, separated from the latter by the Northern Outfall Sewer which it backed onto. It was a straight road, eight track structure and surprisingly spacious, as was the whole site.

Whitelegg 0-6-2T No. 41981 in front of the magnificent coaling stage/water tower at Plaistow in the mid-1950s. It was built as No. 70 *Basildon* for the LT&SR by the North British Locomotive Company in 1903 but the name was removed when renumbered by the Midland Railway as No. 2181. Under the LM&SR it was renumbered to 2221 in 1923 but reverted to No. 2181 in 1939 before becoming No. 1981 in November 1947 and No. 41981 in June 1948; it survived over three years longer than the rest of the class, lasting until the end of LT&S steam in June 1962 although it spent most of this time in store at Tilbury and then Plaistow. There was a messroom for the coalmen underneath the coaling stage and a room which contained all of the Engine Records Cards for the LT&S sheds.

A long-standing Tilbury line engine which also remained in service until June 1962, '3F' 0-6-0T No. 47328 at Plaistow in 1949. The BR number applied in July 1948 is in large 12in. LM&SR-pattern block numerals and the lettering on the tank is in 10in. block. Note the AWS cylinder on top of the tank. At nationalisation, the LT&S had a handful of 'Jinties' to supplement the 0-6-2Ts on goods work but and more arrived in the 1950s, increasing to a maximum of thirteen. In 1956 they were occasionally used on the Upminster-Grays passenger service. No. 47328 was one of the last three on the LT&S when they were withdrawn in June 1962. Plaistow shed was opened in 1911 to replace the original LT&SR shed and had eight roads that could hold forty-eight engines. Its strangest feature was the skeleton wall of the old shed free-standing from the replacement structure.

Half a dozen Midland Railway Johnson '2F' 0-6-0s were based at LT&S sheds at the end of the Second World War and two lasted until April 1957. No. 58200 at Plaistow on 15th March 1953 had been transferred from Kentish Town in February 1951 and was there until withdrawal in June 1954.

Stanier 2-6-4T No. 42502 poses in front of the shed on 23rd March 1957. The first eight three-cylinder 2-6-4Ts were built with domeless boilers and parallel sided bunkers; later engines had domed boilers and bunkers with tapered/sloping sides to improve the movement of coal down the bunker as the fireman used it up, and also improving visibility when working bunker first. Plaistow carried out all boiler washouts and maintenance, apart from very basic procedures, often between an engine bringing an Up morning peak-hour train into Fenchurch Street and returning on a Down train in the evening peak. The water supplied on the LT&S was particularly poor and an expensive 'hot water washing out plant' was installed in the 1920s and a booster pump was added in 1938; even with this the frequency of re-tubing was abnormally high.

The first BR Standard engine to be withdrawn was 2-6-4T No. 80103 after it twisted its frames at the end of 1961. It was condemned in August 1962 and was cut up at Stratford in the following month. No. 80103 was on Plaistow shed in around 1958 with Stanier 3-cylinder 2-6-4T No. 42533 behind. It was only ever on the LT&S, going new to Plaistow in March 1955 and moving to Tilbury in October 1959.

Fairburn No. 42258 and Stanier No. 42522 wait at the shed exit signals in front of another four 2-6-4Ts on 8th July 1959. Plaistow Station was beyond the Sewer bridge on the left of the picture and the shed building is on the far right. In the background to the right of No. 42522 is the mechanical overhead coaling plant which was belatedly installed in 1955. Plaistow was the subject of one of those intriguing tales for which we will never know the full story. On 1st November 1959 the shed officially closed and the majority of its allocation was transferred to Tilbury with the remainder going to Shoeburyness. However, right up to 1962, visitors reported that working steam locomotives continued to use the shed, and boiler washouts and repairs were still chalked up on the boards inside.

East Ham

Stanier three-cylinder 2-6-4T No 42503 leads four other 2-6-4Ts, a BR Standard, a Fairburn, another Stanier three-cylinder and finally another Standard through East Ham en-route to Plaistow shed after taking the stock from their Up Southend trains to Little Ilford Sidings on 1st December 1958.

O.J. Morris/Rail Archive Stephenson

For many decades the class of fourteen 0-6-2Ts were the most common goods engines on the LT&SR and despite the arrival of ten WD 'Austerity' 2-8-0s and ten Gresley 'J39' 0-6-0s they remained in service until the diesels arrived in 1958. No. 41987 at East Ham in the 1950s was one of the last to be withdrawn, in February 1959. It was originally LT&SR No. 76 *Dunton*, and became MR No. 2187 in 1912, LM&SR No. 2227 in 1924, back to No. 2187 in 1939. Finally, it was renumbered as 1987 in October 1947 and then BR No. 41987 in September 1950.

Little Ilford

Stanier 2-6-4T No. 42531 passes Little Ilford No. 3 signal box with an Up train on 29th July 1959. This box dated from 1908 and controlled the Through lines between Barking and East Ham; Little Ilford No. 2 on the opposite side of the tracks worked the Goods lines and the Northern Sidings.

Barking

Barking Station is 7½ miles from Fenchurch Street. The LM&SR undertook major capital expenditure, completed in 1932, under what was termed the 'Southend Scheme', quadrupling the Barking-Upminster section and improving the layout at both ends of Barking Station, and the District Line services were extended from Barking to Upminster. The Local lines between Campbell Junction and Barking had been completely resignalled using semi-automatic two-aspect colour lights between 1927 and 1929 and this system was then installed on the new local lines from Upney to Upminster.

Stanier 2-6-4T No. 2511 approaching Barking with a Fenchurch Street-Southend train on 25th September 1948. It was not renumbered until February 1949. Note the destination board above the bufferbeam – these were discontinued soon after the LT&S was transferred to the Eastern Region in February 1949 – and the two Midland Railway-built coaches at the front. The Tottenham & Forest Gate lines to/from Kentish Town are on the far side, beyond the London Transport District Line tracks.

The LM&SR-designed North British-built 827 bhp Bo-Bo No. 10800 near Barking on 3rd February 1955. It was at Plaistow between 18th December 1954 and 12th February 1955, 'to determine the best method of handling excursion and other passenger trains over the electrified tracks' [post-electrification]. It cost £61,149 when built in June 1950 and had been on the Southern Region since August 1952, although most of the previous eighteen months were spent in Brighton Works from June 1953 until February 1954 and from April until December 1954; after running-in trials it went to Plaistow on 11th December. No. 10800 actually spent the majority of its time on the LT&S on goods work. It moved away to Rugby on 9th February 1955 and remained there until withdrawn in 1959. The similar Type '1' diesels ordered from North British under BR's Modernisation Plan proved equally unreliable and were withdrawn with less than ten years' service.

The '4F' 0-6-0s were the most common motive power for excursion trains to the LT&S seaside resorts during the 1950s. No. 44210 was approaching Barking with a Down train. It was built at Derby and entered traffic in November 1925 and achieved forty years in service. No. 44210 was at Cricklewood from nationalisation, then Kentish Town in November 1949, gained its BR number in January 1950 and moved back to Cricklewood in August 1962. Note the advertising posters – the one on the left is for 'Kit-e-Kat' cat food; now owned by Mars it is still a well-known pet food brand. The one on the right for 'OMO' washing powder which used the strapline 'Adds Brightness' fared less well, although the brand is owned by Unilever and is still used in some countries although, unsurprisingly, it fell out of favour in the UK.

This picture illustrates the need for the extensive track alterations needed at Barking to eliminate conflicting traffic flows of which there were around 700 movements daily over these flat junctions. The work is well underway at the east end of the station as Gresley 'J39' No. 64776 with a freight, probably from Ripple Lane, is about to cross over the LT&S 'Southend Direct' lines on 12th April 1958. The Darlington-built 0-6-0 was at Stratford for a decade up to November 1956 when it moved to Parkeston Quay, remaining there until withdrawn in August 1959.

Fairburn 2-6-4T No. 42255 at the east end of Barking station. Built at Derby in November 1946 and initially allocated to Newton Heath, it moved to the LT&S at Plaistow in October 1947 and stayed there until withdrawal in June 1962. A District Line train is behind No. 42255 and in the background is the Art-Deco style Odeon cinema, opened in 1935 and closed in 1998; a block of flats called 'The Odeon' was then built on the site.

The first Barking Station, dating from 1854, consisted of two platforms only, as rebuilt in 1908 with eight platforms as the District Line electric trains were extended from East Ham to Barking. Further alterations were made in 1932, when the District Line was extended to Upminster. The platforms on the right were used by the London Transport trains and their two-aspect colour signalling contrasts with the semaphore signals on the non-electrified lines. Stanier 2-6-4T No. 42529 passes Barking West signal box as it arrives from London on 7th September 1958.

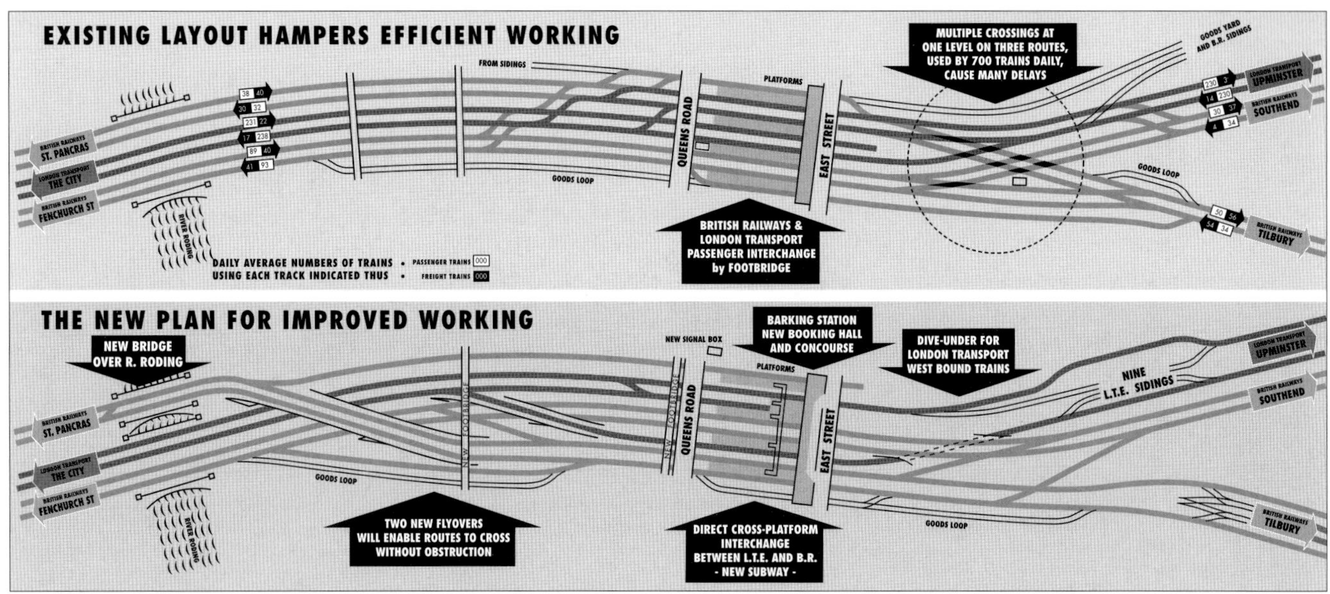

This Eastern Region poster explains the modernisation work at Barking which was carried out at the end of the 1950s as part of the preparation for the LT&S electrification. The aim of the reorganisation was to segregate completely the operation of the London Transport District Line and the Tilbury lines between London and Upminster, removing physical connections between the two and building two flyovers. There would also be cross-platform interchange between the LT and BR lines.

The 12.25pm from Fenchurch Street, headed by Fairburn 2-6-4T No. 42255, is on the Down Fast line and will take the 'Direct' route via Becontree on 12th May 1961. No. 42255 was built at Derby in November 1946 and initially allocated to Newton Heath; it moved to the LT&S at Plaistow in October 1947 and stayed there until withdrawal in June 1962. The Slow lines, leading towards Dagenham Dock and Tilbury are over on the far side, beyond the flyover opened on 11th May 1959 to carry the Up Tilbury traffic onto the Tottenham & Forest Gate (T&FG) line to Gospel Oak, Kentish Town and St. Pancras. In the foreground are the London Transport District/Metropolitan fourth-rail electric lines and nearest is the Down T&FG line. Note the lofty footbridge between Tanner Street and North Street, required because of an old right of way.

Stanier 2-6-4T No. 42514 with a Down train alongside one of the new flyovers which has recently had its first track laid. The tall chimney in the background belonged to the Howard & Sons Ltd chemical factory at Ilford.

BR 2-6-4T No. 80132 approaching Barking station from the west, crossing over the River Roding, probably in 1959. The start of the Barking flyover is on the right. No. 80132 went new to Plaistow in March 1956, moving to Tilbury in October 1959 with most of the other 2-6-4Ts when Plaistow closed.

One of the final batch produced for the Eastern and North Eastern Regions of British Railways, LM&SR-designed twin motor shunter No. 12108 with an English Electric 6KT engine, was the forerunner of the standard BR 350 bhp diesel shunters, it was running round an engineering train standing in Platform 8, the most southerly one, at Barking on 29th March 1959. No. 12108 was built at Darlington in May 1952 and was only ever allocated to Stratford from where it was withdrawn at the end of 1971. As it passes by, the guard-cum-shunter is stowing away his shunting pole into the early LM&SR-built van, by now branded 'not in common use', whilst a PW worker watches on. Brake van No. 357572 was one of a batch of 100 to LM&SR Diagram D1659 which was basically a Midland Railway design built by the Birmingham Railway Carriage & Wagon Co. in 1925, their builder's plate is visible on the solebar.

The LT&SR electrification was not completed until 1961 although the Midland Railway (LT&SR Purchase) Act 1912 included this clause: *'The company shall forthwith prepare a scheme for working traffic by electrical power by the direct route between Fenchurch Street station and Southend-on-Sea ... and ... the company shall carry out and complete such scheme within seven years'.* For a number of reasons, not least the outbreak of the First World War in 1914, the electrification did not proceed and the LM&SR managed to remove the statutory requirement in 1929. Post-war expenditure was concentrated on capacity improvements such as the quadrupling of the line between Barking and Upminster which was completed in 1932 and the remodelling of Fenchurch Street in 1935. Nothing more happened until after nationalisation when a committee was set up in January 1949 *'to outline a scheme of electrification for the LT&S line'* and when it reported in 1950 it recommended 1,500 Volt DC be used on the whole of the LT&S including the Romford-Upminster line and the Thames Haven branch. The scheme was approved in November 1950 but was postponed because of adverse economic conditions and when these improved it was decided that extending the GER Shenfield line electrification to Chelmsford and Southend Victoria, which involved much less expenditure, should take priority. This was completed by the end of 1956 but by then BR had decided to standardise on 25kV electrification and so when eventually work began on the LT&SR this system was used.

The full electric service began in June 1962 using 112 Class 'AM2' four-car high-density sets of the type shown at Barking in the early 1970s, unit No. 302 which under TOPS was a Class '302'. A District Line underground train is just visible to the right of the EMU. In 1961 the station handled about 50,000 passengers each day. Interchange between the LT&S and the District Lines amounted to around 15,000 passengers daily and was facilitated by the cross-platform interchange provided in the new layout. After inauguration of the LT&S electric service all Eastern Region trains ran non-stop between Fenchurch Street or Stepney East and Barking.

Another Class '302', No. 300, departing from Platform 5 at Barking for Fenchurch Street in the 1970s. These four-car units were originally known to railwaymen as 'LTS stock'.

Ripple Lane

Work began on a completely new marshalling yard at Ripple Lane in 1937 to relieve the existing LT&S yards at Little Ilford and Plaistow. It was opened in 1940, and extended from fifteen sidings to twenty-two in around 1950. When British Railways began planning the LT&S electrification in 1950 it had already been decided to close the two old yards and to mechanise Ripple Lane which would become the concentration point for all LT&S line freight. However, work did not begin for several years and it was not until 1957 that the Up and Down main lines were diverted to make way for construction to begin on the new yard. It was partially opened in June 1958, as a 'flat' yard with fifty-one sidings and a capacity of 2,271 wagons, and a diesel depot was opened in November 1959. The full yard with hump working was finally brought into use in March 1961, with the trackwork around the Hump having been rusting away for almost three years. The yard was primarily used to remarshal traffic between LT&S line trip workings and cross-London freights to both the south and north yards. Within a very short time, Ripple Lane became a victim of British Rail's move to more and more block train working and plans were drawn up in 1967 to remove the hump and reduce it to a small flat yard; these were implemented in May 1968. Further change came in 1971 when twelve new sidings were built and the Barking Freightliner Depot was constructed on part of the site. Six of the sidings were out of use by the early 1990s and the diesel depot was closed in 1994.

Brush Type '2' No. D5508 with a westbound freight passes Ripple Lane signal box on 5th August 1960. No. D5508 was at Stratford from December 1959 until September 1960 when it moved to March although it returned there two months later and was withdrawn there in 1980 as No. 31008. Photographs from this period all show the yard as very weedy, which is probably why it was not used in early PR films.

Looking west as BR Sulzer Type '2' No. D5046 runs over the hump on 5th September 1960. It went new to March in October 1959 and was transferred to Stratford in September 1960; it moved back to East Anglia in March 1961. No. D5046 ended its days on the LMR Stoke Division and was withdrawn in July 1976 as TOPS No. 24046. The reception sidings visible under the Renwick Road bridge are largely empty and the tracks are already overgrown with vegetation. The ramp to the right of No. D5046 was the road access to the diesel depot.

North British Locomotive Company diesel-electric Type '2' No. D6116 in front of the short covered four-road re-fuelling section of Ripple Lane depot in April 1960, a few months after it opened. Ten of the class, Nos D6110-D6119, were allocated to Stratford for use on the Great Eastern and LT&S lines. No. D6116 entered service in June 1959 but was reported out of use at Stratford within three months and did not return to traffic until early 1960. It left for the Scottish Region in September 1960 and was one of twenty in the class to be re-engined in 1966, but even then it only lasted until the end of 1971.

A carefully posed picture of the same Type '2' under the futuristic sand-filling facility at the extreme easterly end of the shed. The driver is pretending to fill the sandboxes on the leading bogie.

A Brush Type '2' receives attention over one of the inspection pits inside the depot having been refuelled. The fifteen locomotives of the class based at Ripple Lane for LT&S freight duties went to Stratford for heavy maintenance because the depot was really little more than a covered refuelling shed.

To Tilbury – Purfleet

One man is painting at the front of the signal box while two others paint the level crossing gates, with a fourth acting as lookout, all under the watchful eye of the signalman as BR Standard 2-6-4T No. 80136 approaches Purfleet station with an Up train on 23rd May 1959. It went new to Plaistow in May 1956, moving to Tilbury in October 1959 when that shed officially closed. On the left are the large Thames Board Mills which were rail-served until the 1960s. The firm, which made paper and board, had operated on the site since around 1887 and expanded significantly over the years. It was taken over by the Unilever Group in 1965 but declined over the following decade and production on the site eventually ended in 2004. The travelling cranes on the right moved along a pier which ran out into the Thames; the wharf belonged to Cory's coal merchants but the cranes don't seem too well employed and there are very few wagons in their yard. It is hard to imagine now but huge quantities of coal came by vessel from the North East of England to London and much would be off loaded here. Note the BR Drewry 204 bhp diesel shunter in the yard headshunt behind the signal box and the off-duty 'bobby' about to start his Lambretta LD150 scooter. The signals are pure Midland Railway and the trespass notice by the crossing will be headed up 'Midland Railway' with 'LT&SR Section' in small writing on the second line.

Modernisation is underway as Brush Type '2' No. D5513 runs through with a breakdown train on 25th April 1959. It was always at Stratford, from July 1958 until March 1979. On withdrawal as No. 31013 it went into Departmental stock as a Train Heating Unit, numbered ADB968013, and lasted until January 1983. The rebuilding of the station was completed in late 1961.

Another Stratford Brush Type '2', No. D5516, heads a train of oil tanks from Thames Haven on 25th July 1959. By 1961, fifteen of the class were based at Ripple Lane covering virtually all of the LT&SR freight work, returning to Stratford only for heavy maintenance. No. D5516 was there until November 1967 and returned for its final years up to withdrawal in July 1976 as No. 31016. The lattice footbridge was a typical LT&S design but the arrangement of this one was dictated by its abnormal length; it was replaced in 1961 by a bridge at the level crossing because, as this picture clearly shows, there was insufficient clearance under the overhead wires.

West Thurrock Junction

A view from the bridge east of the junction as a Brush Type '2' approaches West Thurrock Junction with the 12.10pm train of Shell/BP oil tanks from Thames Haven on 21st May 1958. The early locomotives in this class only had the numbers on one cab on each side, preventing identification of the locomotive in this picture. The line on the left is the Down Loop which joined the Down Main opposite the brake van of the train. Grays station is in the distance as is the Thames on the extreme right.

Grays

The tapered bunker of the later Stanier three-cylinder 2-6-4Ts shows up clearly as No. 42509 waits at Grays with an Up train on 30th July 1958. On the left, a Metropolitan-Cammell DMU is working the Upminster service which branched off at West Thurrock Junction. The station building at Grays suffered a direct bomb hit in 1941 and the eastern side had to be demolished but it was not replaced until 1954. The new building was brick-built with a pre-stressed concrete roof which was cantilevered out over the road approach and formed a canopy over the Up platform as can be seen in the right background above the 2-6-4T's train.

This is a 'posed' shot to show two trains running in together past Grays West signal box on 18th June 1959 after the Down siding had been converted into a third line on which the Metro-Cammell Lightweight two-car DMU is standing. On the extreme left is the resident Grays Drewry diesel shunter, No. 11135, the traffic still enough at this date to justify this. The signal box was was supplied by the Railway Signalling Co. in 1900 to replace the original box and was in use until August 1961.

Tilbury Town

Fairburn 2-6-4T No. 42226 approaching Tilbury Town with an Up service on 8th February 1958. It was built at Derby in May 1946 and went straight to Plaistow, moving to Stoke in June 1962. The station was opened in 1886 as 'Tilbury Dock' and remained virtually unaltered until the 1960s electrification; it was renamed as 'Tilbury Town (for Tilbury Docks)' in 1934. In the background between the railway and the ship are extensive warehouses which were all rail-served at this time. Note the blue BR(E) enamels warning passengers to use the footbridge to cross the line.

Tilbury Riverside

The pioneer three-cylinder 2-6-4T No. 42500 leaves Tilbury Riverside station with a train for Barking on 2nd July 1955. It was the only Stanier tank engine saved for preservation and after spending many years at Bressingham Museum moved to the National Railway Museum at York. The train has passed under what became known locally as the Arrol bridge after the contractor Sir William Arrol & Co. Ltd who built it in 1927; it led to the landing stages on the east side of the station. The tracks curving away behind the signal box go to Southend. The signals with corrugated arms and flat tops date from 1927; the route indicators allowed the multiple arms on their predecessor 1906 signals to be reduced to a single arm.

Midland Railway '1P' 0-4-4T No. 58054 at Tilbury Riverside in 1954 was a regular performer on the Romford - Grays push-pull service; in 1955 seven of these trains each day ran through to Tilbury. No. 58054 was allocated to Plaistow from November 1951 onwards and was withdrawn in November 1955. The station was plain 'Tilbury' until the 1930s when 'Riverside' was added. The Ferry Road (Arrol) bridge is in the background.

LT&SR Whitelegg 0-6-2T No. 41987 shunting at Tilbury Riverside on 8th February 1958, a year before it was withdrawn. Built by the North British Locomotive Co. in 1908 as LT&SR No. 76 *Dunton* it became MR No. 2187 in 1912, LM&SR No. 2227 in 1924 and reverted to No. 2187 in 1939. Finally, it was renumbered as 1987 in October 1947 to make way for new Fairburn 2-6-4Ts. The absence of a smokebox number plate was apparently due to Bow Works, which maintained all the ex-LT&SR engines, being unable to produce the BR cast plates and although they were ordered from Derby they somehow were not fitted. Note the AWS cylinder on the tank top; this was the only class of ex-Midland Railway engines that were all fitted with this equipment.

Boat trains ran between St. Pancras and Tilbury Riverside for shipping lines such as P&O, Orient Line and Swedish Lloyd from the end of the nineteenth century until early 1963. They travelled via the Tottenham & Forest Gate Joint line to join the LT&S at Woodgrange Park near Barking. At Tilbury West Junction Ivatt Class '4' 2-6-0 No. 43120 takes away empty stock from a boat train arrival at Riverside on Sunday 19th July 1959. It had propelled the train out of the station past East Junction and pulled forward round the triangle past the shed in order to avoid using a station pilot or running round. Cricklewood Shed had a handful of the 2-6-0s which were mainly used on transfer freight work but turned their hand to passenger duties when required and often hauled the boat trains to Tilbury. A line of dead ex-LT&SR tanks on the shed is visible in the right background.

204 bhp diesel shunter No. D2211 at Tilbury South signal box takes the stock of an incoming train out of Riverside Station on 18th July 1959. It was built in September 1954 as No. 11112, became No. D2211 a week before this photograph was taken, and was allocated to Stratford between August 1955 and December 1959. It was acting as station pilot during the period when the station was being prepared for electrification as can be seen in the foreground. Tilbury South signal box was built in 1906 and apart from its 18ft width, needed to accommodate two frames, was a standard product of the Railway Signal Company. It was replaced in September 1961 by a new panel box at Tilbury which also took over from the North Junction box.

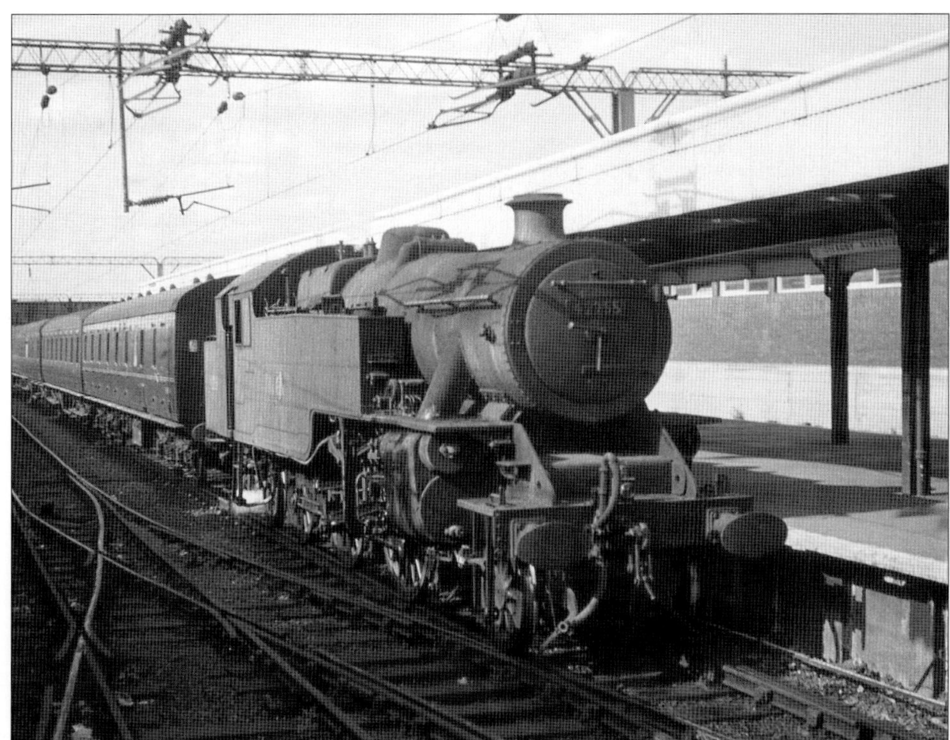

Fairburn 2-6-4T No. 42255 in 1962 after arrival at Tilbury Riverside; the overhead equipment had been installed in 1961. Built in November 1946 and originally allocated to the LM&SR Central Division, No. 42255 was one of ten of the class transferred from there to the LT&S in late-1947. Tilbury had been a passenger ferry terminal since the early twentieth century but declined after World War Two and when the Dartford Tunnel opened in 1963 and the passenger service was drastically reduced. Freight traffic was withdrawn from May 1968 and the passenger service in November 1992. Note the station name on the lamp diffusers; these replaced short-lived BR totems.

Tilbury Shed

The shed, which was built in around 1907, was situated in the triangle of the lines formed just north of Riverside station and was provided with a turntable despite this position. It was a spacious straight road shed with four tracks, but rather unusually for the LT&SR, was not of brick construction, but used corrugated iron. The LM&SR modernised it with a coal hoist under another lightly constructed shed. There were plans to house diesel locomotives and the DMUs for the Upminster branch here from the early 1950s but by that stage the shed building was in appalling condition. The Eastern Region finally re-built the shed in 1956/7 with a completely new frame and corrugated asbestos cladding but its role in providing freight engines was soon taken over by Ripple Lane. Electrification made it wholly redundant in June 1962 when it lost its allocation. Since it was a new structure it was not immediately abandoned, remaining available for visiting engines for a short period afterwards.

Displaying its newly painted 33A Tilbury shed plate Whitelegg 0-6-2T No. 41983 is on the ash road shunt duty on 6th June 1954. It was built by the North British Locomotive Company in 1903 as LT&SR No. 72 *Hadleigh*, becoming No. 2183 in 1913, No. 2223 in 1913, No. 2183 in 1939 and finally No. 1983 in 1947 before receiving its BR number in July 1948. Note that its steam heat pipe has been removed for the summer and the smokebox door displays the bolts from the short-lived fixing of a number plate. Behind it is the coaling shed built by the LM&SR in 1936.

Another Whitelegg 0-6-2T No. 41989 stands inside the dilapidated shed sometime in the 1950s. It was the last of the ten engines built by North British and started life as LT&SR No. 78 *Dagenham Dock* before going through the same renumbering cycle as No. 41983 above. Facilities were basic here, but it was surprising what a skilled fitter could do armed with a bench, vice and a few basic tools. The LT&SR freight tanks were mostly allocated to Plaistow, with just the odd one officially outbased at Tilbury, but because of the nature of the traffic and the important local docks there were always a number of the fourteen strong class to be found on shed here at the weekends.

Ex-Great Northern Railway 'C12' 4-4-2T No. 67363 rests in the yard between duties on 24th January 1957. It came to Tilbury to work the Upminster-Grays push-pull after its previous employment on the 'Annesley Dido' between Annesley and Bulwell Common ended in September 1956. No. 67363 stayed for just under two years before being despatched to New England for Peterborough station pilot duties.

East Tilbury

4-4-2T No. 41939 at an almost deserted East Tilbury in the early 1950s was built by Nasmyth, Wilson & Co. for the LM&SR as No. 2121 in 1925 but was not renumbered to No. 41939 until November 1949. It was allocated to Plaistow until withdrawal in February 1959. The station which was on the line from Tilbury to Pitsea was on the Tilbury side of Muckingford crossing, between Low Street and Stanford-le-Hope, was opened as 'East Tilbury Halt' in September 1936 after a new shoemaking factory and company village was built nearby. The 550ft long timber platforms were built on concrete piers and each had a small flat-roofed timber shelter. The word 'Halt' was dropped from the name in February 1949.

Thames Haven

Another picture of No. 41939 in the 1950s, this time at Thames Haven goods station, which was right at the end of the Thames Haven branch. The single ex-Great Eastern Railway corridor coach suggests this was an unadvertised workmen's train. The four-mile long branch was opened in June 1855 by the Thames Haven Dock & Railway Company but was purchased by the LT&SR the following month. The docks never materialised and there were merely wharves along the river. It would not be until the early twentieth century that the branch began to develop with the building of a number of private sidings including one for Anglo-Saxon Petroleum Co. (which became Shell in 1955) which was the precursor to the line's later development for oil traffic from the installations at Thames Haven, Shell Haven and Coryton from the late 1950s. By 1961 there were around 1,300 tank wagons originating from the branch every week.

Romford - Upminster - Grays

A single line branch from Romford to Grays via Upminster was opened in 1892. As large-scale suburban development reached the Romford-Hornchester-Upminster area by the 1930s, the LM&SR bowed to local pressure to improve the service and introduced push-pull trains in 1934. These were worked by three Midland Railway Johnson '1P' 04-4Ts, and there were now thirty trains each way between Romford and Upminster, although the Upminster-Grays service remained unchanged. In the late 1940s the line effectively became two separate branches when through working from Romford to Grays/Tilbury ended.

'1P' 0-4-4T No. 58038 at Upminster with the Romford push-pull on 17th April 1954. The Midland Railway veteran from 1876, which had been at Upminster since 1934 and was renumbered from No. 1261 in January 1948, had just two months to remain in service. It was replaced by No. 58091 transferred from Wellingborough and the three Upminster 0-4-4Ts continued to operate the branch service until the end of 1955 when 'N7' 0-6-2Ts were brought in to replace them. No. 58038 is in the 'Branch' through platform, a bi-directional line which dated from the 1932 remodelling for the District Line extension. The engine shed behind No. 58038 was also built in 1932 to replace the old shed which had to be demolished to make way for the new local lines. It had been opened in around 1885 in anticipation of the building of the Grays and Romford branches; the new shed was itself closed in September 1956.

After the 0-4-4Ts were withdrawn, several push-pull fitted 'N7/2' 0-6-2Ts and a GNR 'C12' 4-4-2T arrived in 1956 for the branch services. Two of the 0-6-2Ts were on shed at Upminster on 21st May 1956, both built by Beardmores for the L&NER in August 1927 and transferred to Plaistow but sub-shedded at Upminster in January 1956. When Upminster shed was closed from 17th September, its allocation was transferred to Tilbury. On the left is No. 69691 which moved away to Stratford in October 1957 and on the right is No. 69695 which followed it in September 1958. The latter worked the final timetabled steam train on the Romford-Upminster section, the 6.13pm from Romford, on Saturday, 15th September 1956. One of the three-coach push-pull sets is in the siding on the left.

The driver of a Derby Lightweight DMU hands over the staff for the line from Upminster to the West Thurrock Junction signalman on 9th March 1958, only ten weeks after the diesel units had taken over the working of the Upminster-Grays section. They brought a greatly improved service, with twenty-nine weekday trains to Grays, eight to Tilbury and two to Ockendon. The single line was controlled by the Railway Signal Company electric train staff with trains crossing at Ockendon.

Two visitors make their way down the steps of Upminster East signal box as 4-4-2T No. 41978 leaves with the 11am train to Grays on 30th November 1957. No. 41978 was built at Derby as late as March 1930, the last of the 'Tilbury tanks'. It was LM&SR No. 2160 until May 1948 when it was renumbered into the 419xx series to make way for new Fairburn 2-6-4Ts. No. 41978 was allocated to Plaistow from 1952 until withdrawn in February 1959. After the closure of Upminster shed in 1956 and the withdrawal of the 0-4-4Ts, the 4-4-2Ts although not push-pull fitted, were occasionally used on the Upminster-Grays trains.
K.L. Cook/Rail Archive Stephenson

A new concrete footbridge is already in place and posts for the overhead masts have started to be erected as Stanier 2-6-4T No. 42502 sets off from Ockendon towards Upminster on 8th May 1960.

A Metro-Cammell Lightweight two-car DMU waits to leave Ockendon for Upminster on 19th January 1961. Both these and the Derby Lightweight units were used on the line until electrification of the Upminster-Grays section in 1963. The Romford-Upminster service was proposed for closure under the Beeching Plan. However, the Romford-Upminster Branch Line Users' Association was set up and successfully fought off the closure, and the line was electrified in 1986 to eliminate what had become an isolated pocket of DMU operation.

To Southend and Shoeburyness

Chalkwell

Fairburn 2-6-4T No. 42223 at Chalkwell on a train to Shoeburyness in the 1950s. Built in April 1946, it went straight to the LT&S and stayed there until withdrawn in June 1962; this picture was taken while it was allocated to Tilbury, between July 1951 and November 1956. Chalkwell Station was opened in 1933 with platforms alongside the sea (officially 'sand and mud' according to OS maps); it was originally intended to be a halt but instead was built as a complete station with waiting rooms, parcels facilities, etc.

112 Class 'AM2' four-car high-density sets were built for the LT&S and all were delivered by mid-1960 and pending completion of the electrification most were put into store, although some were used on the Great Eastern line to Colchester and Clacton. Limited peak-hour running began in November 1961. Like all the Eastern Region AC EMUs of the period, they were equipped to operate on both 25kV AC and the reduced 6.25kV voltage in the inner London areas where headroom for the overhead wires was reduced. On the LT&S the changeover point was just east of Barking station on both the Upminster and Tilbury routes. They quickly ran into problems and failures became common; after investigation they were traced back to problems with the voltage changeover equipment and modifications were made. With Driving Trailer No. E75275 leading, unit No. 302 approaches Chalkwell on 6th October 1965.

On the same day as the previous photograph, another 'AM2', set No. 282 with No. E75330 at the front, leaves Chalkwell on a Fenchurch Street service. When the LT&S was electrified in 1961, a new form of four-character codes was introduced. The first digit represented the train classification, the second character the route with the third and fourth digits the individual train number; '12-56' indicated an Up train running via Upminster. Classed as '302' under TOPS, the 'AM2' sets increasingly showed their age and all were withdrawn by 1998.

Nine four-car 'AM 8/2' units were built at York for the LT&S for use on the traffic arising from cruise liners calling at Tilbury. They were similar to the three-car 'AM 8/1' sets built in 1959 for the Great Eastern line suburban services. With Driving Trailer No. E75958 leading, unit No. 318 has just left Chalkwell on a service to Tilbury, also on 6th October 1965. The 'AM 8/2' units had a dedicated motor luggage van, the third vehicle in this picture, with a pantograph and a BR coaching stock roundel, which enabled them to be used for parcels and mail in off-peak periods. The EMUs replaced the Swedish Lloyd boat trains from St. Pancras in April 1963. Tilbury declined as a cruise port with the merged P&O and Orient Line moving its operation to Southampton in 1969 and in 1971 four of the units had the MLVs converted into brake seconds; the units became Class '308/2' under TOPS.

Upminster

Upminster Station had been extensively improved in the early 1930s with a new bay for Grays Branch trains and an additional island platform. A large amount of remodelling was done in 1957 to separate the British Railways and London Transport tracks. An additional platform, No. 6, was built for the Romford trains, where the Derby Lightweight DMU is standing on the day it was opened, 20th July 1957. A contingent of PW workers appear to be putting the finishing touches to the trackwork as the unit is signalled to leave for Romford. Platforms 3, 4 and 5 were used by the London Transport District Line trains.

Stanier three-cylinder 2-6-4T No. 42524 leaves Upminster with the 12 noon Fenchurch Street to Shoeburyness on 21st July 1957.

K.L. Cook/Rail Archive Stephenson

Stanier 2-6-4T No. 42517 departs from Upminster with a Down train in 1962. The overhead wires are in place and new 'lozenge'-shaped signs have replaced the BR totems. The station had been extensively rebuilt in 1932 as part of the quadrupling of the Barking-Upminster section and the extension of District Line trains to Upminster. All of the platforms were lengthened to 700ft to accommodate the Fenchurch Street trains; the shaped reinforced concrete sections show up clearly in front of No. 42517.

Laindon

WD 'Austerity' 2-8-0 No. 90196 with an engineering train at Laindon on 27th October 1957. It had arrived on the LT&S allocated to Plaistow in May 1955, one of several 'Austerities' brought in to handle the growing goods LT&S traffic. The *Railway Observer* reported *'Duties allocated to the 2-8-0 Cl. 8F (W.D.) engines stationed at Plaistow include the following freight workings: 12.10am (MX) 12.45am (Suns.) Dagenham Dock to Temple Mills; 2.10am (MX and Suns.) Ripple Lane to Temple Mills; 11.17pm (SX) Purfleet to Thames Wharf.'* When Plaistow closed in November 1959 No. 90196 moved to Tilbury for its last three years in service. The station received significant improvements under the 'Southend Scheme' in 1933/4 with an extra platform face, lengthened platforms and additional carriage sidings and goods yard sidings.

The railwaymen at Laindon are looking for inspiration after BR 2-6-4T No. 80097 has failed while working the 3.25pm Fenchurch Street to Shoeburyness on 28th July 1957. As part of the pre-electrification work, the station was altered in 1957 to improve operational flexibility and the platforms were extended; the work was not completed until November as this picture shows. *K.L. Cook/Rail Archive Stephenson*

Another BR 2-6-4T comes to the rescue. No. 80100 has just made a special stop at Laindon with the following 4pm Fenchurch Street to Shoeburyness to pick up the passengers from the failed 80097's train. Fortunately, it is outside the peak hour so hopefully they all managed to fit on! No. 80097 was delivered new to Plaistow from Brighton Works in December 1954 and was followed in January by No. 80100; both transferred to Tilbury in November 1959. They were part of a batch of ten new BR Standard 2-6-4Ts, Nos 80096-80105, sent to the LT&S between November 1954 and April 1955 as replacements for Fairburn engines Nos 42230/1/2/48-53/6 which were transferred to Neasden to replace a similar number of Thompson 'L1' 2-6-4 tanks on the Marylebone and Metropolitan commuter services. *K.L. Cook/Rail Archive Stephenson*

Pitsea

4-4-2T No. 41967 departs from Pitsea with a Down Sunday train on 26th September 1948. Built in 1909 by Robert Stephenson & Hawthorn Ltd as LT&SR No. 81 *Aveley*, renumbered by the Midland Railway in 1912 as 2178, it was renumbered again by the LM&SR to No. 2149 in 1929 and finally became BR No. 41967 in April 1948; it was withdrawn from Tilbury in November 1952. The station was named 'Pitsea for Vange' in 1932 but reverted to plain 'Pitsea' in 1952; Vange was a village to the east of Pitsea. Note the LM&SR platform-mounted signal, Midland Railway lamp post and gas lamp case and the rake of LT&SR-built coaches in the background.

Fairburn 2-6-4T No. 42218 at Pitsea with the 2.44pm to Tilbury on 17th April 1954. Pitsea became a junction where the original line from Tilbury to Southend met the 'Direct' line between Barking and Upminster which had been opened in 1888. In the right background is the LM&SR signal box, built in 1934 when a new engine spur was provided on the site of the 1888 box at the east end of the Tilbury line platforms to allow an engine on a train from Tilbury terminating at Pitsea to run round without fouling the main line.

'4F' 0-6-0 No. 44297 is emitting lots of black smoke as it works a return excursion back to the London Midland Region on 28th June 1959. It was at Plaistow prior to nationalisation, moving to Kentish Town at the end of 1951 and then on to Cricklewood in March 1952 until 1962 when it left for Wellingborough. The train is approaching the east end of the Down Upminster line platform which had been extended in 1952 to avoid the need for trains stopping there to draw up twice. In 1956 the junction had been re-laid with switch diamonds to allow Upminster trains to run through at 60mph prior to ascending the steep gradient beyond the station. The large sign on the right refers to the Pitsea Electrical Traction Engineer's Maintenance Depot which in fact was never built.

Benfleet

Electrification work is well underway as Stanier 2-6-4T No. 42520 departs with an Up train from Benfleet on 27th August 1960. Benfleet was the last station rebuilt under the LT&SR, opening in December 1911. The station and station master's house were in stock brick finished with blue facings and rough casting.

Main-line diesels were rarely used on LT&S passenger services even in the brief period up to electrification. Brush Type '2' No. D5508 approaches Benfleet with the 12.10pm Shoeburyness-Fenchurch Street on 3rd July 1960. It was at Stratford for most of its working life, including between December 1959 and September 1960. On withdrawal in 1980 as No. 31008 it went into Departmental stock for two years as a Train Heating Unit, numbered ADB968016.

Leigh-on-Sea

4-4-2T No. 41977 with an Up train of Midland Railway coaches at Leigh-on-Sea on 19th July 1952. It was one of the LM&SR-built engines to the Whitelegg design, entering service as No. 2159 in March 1930; was renumbered in April 1948 and worked on the LT&SR until withdrawn in February 1959. The 'new' station was opened in January 1934, replacing an earlier station under an agreement made in 1924 with Southend Corporation to improve both passenger and goods facilities. One unique feature, visible to the right of No. 41977, was a 'cockle' shed at the London end of the Up platform where shellfish to be conveyed by passenger train were left.

Kentish Town '4F' No. 44297 approaching the site of the old station at Leigh-on-Sea with an excursion to Southend on 19th July 1952. In May 1935 the LM&SR Mechanical & Electrical Committee recommended the expenditure of £28,500 for installation of the Hudd system of ATC on the LT&S section, the Ministry of Transport having approved it on a trial basis. It was ordered that all locomotives likely to be used on the line be fitted and a number of '4F' 0-6-0s received the equipment at Bow Works. The system was not brought into use until the end of 1947 and from 1948 only Hudd-fitted engines like No. 44297 were allowed to work over the LT&S.

After the end of the Second World War, the Stanier and Fairburn 2-6-4Ts were usually accompanied by a couple of the Fowler variety. One of these, No. 42374 heads west from Leigh-on-Sea, past Cottage Place between the old and new stations on 9th August 1952. Along with No. 42328 it was at Plaistow from October 1948 until February 1954 when they both moved to Neasden as new BR Standard 2-6-4Ts were delivered.

An excursion to Southend passes over the level crossing which was at the end of the old station's platforms, the traces of which are still visible, on 3rd August 1958. It is hauled by No. 43964, a Midland Railway '4F' 0-6-0 built by Armstrong, Whitworth in 1921, which was at Kentish Town from March 1946 until August 1962 when it moved to Cricklewood. The Up platform of the old station was demolished at the end of 1953 to allow the lines to be slewed outwards to reduce the sharp curve and eliminate the 'S' curve on the eastern approach. The railings on the left along the stub of the old platform separated off an area leased to the 3rd Chalkwell Bay Sea Scouts from around 1936 until 1957.

Westcliff-on-Sea

An interesting street scene along Station Road Westcliff-on-Sea with a café and a garage occupying only the same frontage as the small shops next to it. The garage sells Esso petrol, dispensed from two pumps, but appears to be quite progressive with a sign for 'Self-Drive' cars. In front, BR Standard 2-6-4T No. 80098 leaves with an Up service in around 1960; it went new to Plaistow in September 1954, moving to Tilbury in October 1959. The LT&SR in common with other railways, particularly in the south east, helped develop new residential areas which were financed either wholly or partly by private developers of the land. Westcliff-on-Sea station was opened in 1895 to serve a new housing development to the west of Southend on property owned by the Brassey family. The area soon became built up and the station became busy with London commuter traffic. The signal box visible above the first coach had a 25-lever frame but only nine were ever used.

Southend-on-Sea Central

The bay platforms and carriage sidings are all full of coaches on a Sunday afternoon as Stanier 2-6-4T No. 42506 backs out from Platform 1, the bay on the Down side of the station, on 3rd August 1958. This was the original terminus of the line in 1856 and it became a through station when the line was extended to Shoeburyness in 1884. The station was extended several times, notably in 1899 when two more platforms were added to accommodate the summer excursion traffic together with two carriage sidings; the goods facilities were expanded and the track layout completely revised. There were now four bays for terminating trains and apart from extensions to all the platforms at the west end in 1954 and modernisation of the station buildings in 1957, there was little change until electrification work started in 1959.

Stanier 3-cylinder 2-6-4T No. 42533 waits at Southend Central with the 9.5am to Fenchurch Street in early 1960. It was built in November 1934 and was allocated to Plaistow until World War Two during which it moved away from the LT&S section to Normanton, Leeds, Royston and Saltley. No. 42533 returned to Plaistow in October 1945 and was transferred to Shoeburyness in November 1956 and was withdrawn from there in June 1962.

Southend-on-Sea East

Fairburn 2-6-4T No. 42254 arriving at Southend East with a Shoeburyness train on 31st July 1960. Built in November 1946, it was at Newton Heath until September 1947 when it arrived at Plaistow and worked on the LT&S until withdrawn in June 1962, transferring to Tilbury in November 1959. Opened in 1932, the station was not part of the 1929 'Southend' scheme but was built under Government Loan finance as a terminus for excursion traffic to relieve Southend Central. It was also used from the start for a few peak hour arrivals and departures. Originally there were two through platforms and an Up Main platform, but a Down Main platform was quickly added in early 1933. In practice, the new station was rarely used for excursions with day-trippers opting to enjoy the walk down the High Street from Central Station to the pier. It was renamed 'Southend-on-Sea East' in May 1949 but reverted to 'Southend East' in February 1969.

Thorpe Bay

Stanier 2-6-4T No. 42516 sets off from Thorpe Bay with an Up service on 3rd August 1958. The LT&SR in common with other railways, particularly in the south east, helped develop new residential areas which were financed either wholly or partly by private developers of the land. Thorpe Bay was the last of these built before the Midland Railway takeover and was opened in 1910 with the Thorpe Hall estate providing the land and paying for the construction of the station. It was originally to be named 'Southchurch-on-Sea' but was changed to 'Thorpe Bay' within three weeks after pressure from the estate. There was little development until after the First World War.

Shoeburyness

The town of Shoeburyness did not exist until the 1860s when the War Office moved their Woolwich gun ranges from Plumstead marshes to 'Shoebury Ness', in the South Shoebury parish. The first station was opened in 1884 and was extended in 1910 when six additional carriage sidings were added bringing the total to ten. After the Midland Railway takeover three more were provided together with improved carriage cleaning facilities. Further improvements were made in 1921 when the lines around the sidings were remodelled and a new signal box built. Fairburn 2-6-4T No. 42223 arrives at Shoeburyness on 18th April 1954. Built in April 1946, it went straight to the LT&S and stayed there until withdrawn in June 1962. This picture was taken while it was allocated to Tilbury, between July 1951 and November 1956. The headshunt at the entrance to the carriage sidings is on the left and Shoeburyness Park on the right.

Stanier 2-6-4T No. 42511 waits at Shoeburyness on 1st June 1957. Beyond the footbridge is the mechanical coaling plant dating from 1933 and to its left is the signal box which was built in 1921 when the track layout was remodelled. The bracket signals are LM&SR tubular design dating from the late 1930s, but the wooden post with its short calling-on arm and banner repeater is far more interesting, dating from Midland Railway days or perhaps even earlier.

Stanier 2-6-4T No. 42515 runs into the carriage sidings which were alongside to the south of the approach lines (on the right of the photograph) on 2nd August 1960. By this date Shoeburyness had no less than thirty-one carriage sidings and a mechanical washing plant; it was the principal carriage depot for the stock for the Southend service.

Shoeburyness Shed

The first engine shed at Shoeburyness was built in 1890 and was extended in 1896 when a substantial two-road brick building, of similar design to other LT&SR sheds was constructed between the passenger platforms and the shed itself; a 60ft turntable replaced the original 42ft one to cater for tender engines arriving on excursions. In 1934 an additional two road steel-framed shed alongside the brick-built structure was added as part of the LM&SR modernisation programme which also saw the installation of a water softening plant and a 100 ton mechanised coaling stage. By the post war period the LM&SR-built part of the shed was badly dilapidated so it was again rebuilt with asbestos cladding as a precursor to the similar work done at Tilbury. Shoeburyness Shed did not only service locally terminating trains; there were only minimal water and coal 'top up' facilities at Southend and therefore most engines were diagrammed to return to the depot including those off incoming excursions.

The close proximity of the shed to the station is shown here as Fairburn 2-6-4T No. 42231 stands in the yard in around 1953. It left the LT&S for Neasden at the end of January 1955. The ancient station running in board is pure LT&SR, the station is still illuminated by town gas and the state of the platform without any coping slabs is interesting. Washing day must have been challenging to the residents of Wakering Avenue before electrification.

The photographer has leant over the edge of the platform to take this shot of Fairburn 2-6-4T No. 42257 with the mechanised coaling plant in the left background. Built at Derby in November 1946, it went to Newton Heath for its first year in service, moving to Plaistow in October 1947. The engine records do not show it moving to 27D, the ex-Lancashire & Yorkshire Railway shed at Wigan, although the plate on its smokebox indicates otherwise!

Shoeburyness Shed on 16th November 1962, almost six months after it closed on 16th June, with numerous withdrawn 2-6-4Ts, many partially cannibalised and waiting to be taken away for scrap. The shed was remodelled in 1933/4 when a mechanical coaling plant was installed and a two-road steel framed shed with corrugated roof (on the right of the shed nearest the platform) was added alongside the existing LT&SR brick-built shed. It was re-clad by British Railways but remained in a poor state of repair. The site including the coaling plant was destined for imminent demolition, but the turntable and some water columns were retained and a new rudimentary coaling stage constructed in order to service LMR engines arriving with excursion trains. Of course, this only lasted for a few more years.

The end of the line on 3rd August 1958. Unlike all the other LT&SR stations, Shoeburyness had a wooden station building which dated from when the station was opened in 1884 and is still in use today. On the left is the steel-framed section of the shed which dated back to 1933 that was re-roofed in the 1950s, but was by 1960 so badly decayed that most of it had to be removed completely. The platform level raised walkway behind the buffer stops had recently been built, allowing passengers to reach the Down platform without having to go via the street.

Class '302' EMU No. 263 alongside another EMU in the 1970s. These four-car units were built in 1958 for the London, Tilbury & Southend line electrification and soldiered on until the 1990s. The short canopy on the main station building had to be cut back in 1989 when the overhead line voltage was changed from 6.25kV to 25kV.